WINTERHIKES
IN PUGET SOUND & THE OLYMPIC FOOTHILLS

WINTERHIKES
IN PUGET SOUND & THE OLYMPIC FOOTHILLS

mostly snow-free trails
from lowland forests to summit views

BOBMOOERS

SASQUATCH BOOKS
SEATTLE

For Jill Fugate: Mother, teacher, wife, quilter, hiker, friend, and mountaineer.
Regrettably, for my part, it took her final blending
with the earth to realize the extent to which she was loved.

~

Printed in the United States of America
Distributed in Canada by Raincoast Books, Ltd.
02 01 00 99 98   5 4 3 2 1

Cover and interior design and composition: Kate Basart
Cover photograph: Michael Melford/The Image Bank
Backcover photograph: Bob Mooers
Interior photographs: Bob Mooers
Mapmaker: John Zilly

Library of Congress Cataloging in Publication Data
Mooers, Robert L.
        Winter hikes in Puget Sound & the Olympic foothills : mostly snow-free trails from lowland forests to summit views / Bob Mooers.
                p.   cm.
        ISBN: 1-57061-149-1
        1. Hiking—Washington (State)—Puget Sound Region—Guidebooks. 2. Hiking—Washington (State)—Olympic Mountains—Guidebooks. 3. Trails—Washington (State)—Puget Sound Region—Guidebooks. 4. Trails—Washington (State)—Olympic Mountains—Guidebooks. 5. Puget Sound Region (Wash.)—Guidebooks. 6. Olympic Mountains (Wash.)—Guidebooks. I. Title.
        GV854.5.W33B53 1998
        917.9704'43—dc21   98-28096

IMPORTANT NOTE: Please use common sense. No guidebook can act as a substitute for experience, careful planning, the right equipment, and appropriate training. There is inherent danger in all the activities described in this book, and readers must assume full responsibility for their own actions and safety. Changing or unfavorable conditions in weather, roads, trails, snow or avalanche conditions, waterways, and so forth cannot be anticipated by the author or publisher, but should be considered by any outdoor participants. The author and publisher will not be responsible for the safety of users of this guide.

SASQUATCH BOOKS
615 Second Avenue
Seattle, WA 98104
(206) 467-4300
www.SasquatchBooks.com
books@SasquatchBooks.com

Sasquatch Books publishes high-quality adult nonfiction and children's books related to the Northwest (Alaska to San Francisco). For more information about Sasquatch Books titles, contact us at the address above, or view our site on the World Wide Web.

Contents

Winter Hikes

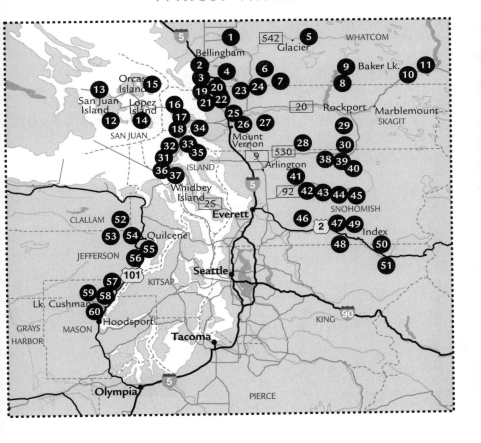

Acknowledgments

Although a single name appears on the cover of this collection of hikes, the book would not exist without the help of many people. Numerous Forest Service personnel responded with caring patience to my many inquiries, as did residents on the fringe of rural civilization when I needed to locate "that old road" to Nameless Mountain.

Much appreciated proofreading and manuscript critique came from Cele Gale and Jill Fugate. Steve Lecocq, of the Whatcom County Parks Department, was kind enough to share with me a budding multi-agency trails masterplan for Chuckanut Mountain. And, when I put out a call for other folk's favorite winter hikes, John Roper, Fred Beavon, and Fred Darvill responded with lists that could lead to volume two.

Another kind of help, in response to my cyber-panic calls eighteen hours a day, came from Teresa McDonald. She talked me down on more than one word-processing emergency.

Introduction

This guide is the happy child of beneficial frustration.

From June to October, I spend a good part of my leisure hours on lofty ridges and sunny summits in the Cascades and Olympics. (Well, airy if not sunny.) Think of it as rest and relaxation from the stresses of work-week hours, or gaining humility from the physical immensity and mind-numbing presence of cherished mountains.

From October to June, however, I wait, with you, for the cold and the storms to recede, taking with them their child, Snow. Of course, there are hundreds of miles of lowland trails for enjoyable winter walks. Waterfalls have a fascination all of their own, a lake is a welcome interlude in the enclosure of deep forest, and an estuary puts one up close to birds and animals, our earth-siblings. I enjoy them all, but none is even a close stand-in for the view from Cascade Pass or a flower-freshened meadow at 5000 feet.

As fall comes on, I find myself pushing aside family and business affairs in order to get in one more weekend up high before freezing levels tumble. Then it's bring on the substitutes. Every Friday night the pattern is the same:

"You wanna hike tomorrow?"

"Sure, where?"

"I was hoping you had a suggestion."

"Me? It was my idea to go. You say where."

"How about Whatsit Lake?"

"Are you crazy? We've been there nine times!"

You get the picture: frustration.

Then I heard the beneficial part of the call: Do something about it yourself. I reasoned that someone in, say, Marysville, would happily drive sixty-five miles for a newly discovered view hike in Whatcom County, if it was doable in the snowy season. I surely would, if it were the other way around. So I put together a list of my favorites in the north Puget Sound counties, hiked them all again, and wrote them up to share.

Field checking all of these, plus finding lots more on my own (poor me) solved my snowy season hiking problem. If you suffer from the same complaint, I hope this guide solves yours.

Hiking in the Snowy Season

When we put "winter" and "hiking" into the same title, some qualifying is in order.

Hiking is basically walking done with specialized clothing and footwear. Unlike rock or ice climbing, or even off-trail mountaineering, hiking usually does not require one to carry technical equipment to survive. Adding "winter" into the mix, however, forces us to put a stronger emphasis on preparedness and safety.

In the mountains of western Washington, the "snowy season" extends roughly from October to the end of June, fully two-thirds of the year. During that time, anything much over 3,000 feet in elevation is likely to have snow, or have had some snow dropped on it. How much snow depends on the severity of the winter and the weather conditions that spring. It also depends on how close the destination in question is to higher mountains or to the moderating effects of marine air. For example, the 2,400-foot summit of Mount Constitution, on Orcas Island, collects considerably less winter white than a peak of similar elevation nearer the Cascade crest.

So, What Is Snowy Season Hiking?

Snowy season hiking is venturing out into the hills from October to June and hiking up to, and over, the snowline, while remaining on recognizable trail. When the trail can no longer be followed with certainty, the outing has ceased to be a hike and has become wilderness navigation.

The snowy season begins around mid fall and extends through deep winter. It is that period of time when snow has not yet obliterated all the trails, though it threatens to do so almost daily. The snowy season continues in different form from spring into early summer, when melting allows trails to reappear. Much depends on elevation. While many trails below 2,000 feet are snow-free much of the year, those above 4,000 feet are rarely identifiable December through April, or even into May and June. Further, since there are winters when Seattle has ten inches of snow upon its streets, it should be apparent that many of the hikes in this book will not always be snow-free. Call Forest Service stations, know the weather forecast, and have a Plan B in mind.

Whether a hike is doable or not in snowy season hinges on more than snow depth and trail visibility. On an infrequently traveled trail, or one on a steep slope, even an inch or two of snow can make it unsafe. On popular trails, substantial accumulations of the white stuff may be packed by boot traffic to the point that the way is plain and safe. However, when old snow-pack bridges a stream or even small creek, or covers downed trees or boulders, it is very easy, especially during spring melt, for a boot-clad human foot to punch through, resulting in anything from an icy wet landing to a serious sprain. And, regardless of trail conditions, if snow begins to fall, it is best to head back.

Safety and Preparation

Clothing and Equipment Essentials

The theme that runs through preparedness for any hiking trip should be packing what you *might* need rather than only those items you know you *will* need. It is far from alarmist to advocate emergency readiness for one or more nights in the woods.

Winter hiking calls for an expanded list of the traditional ten essentials. Following is what this author considers to be the twenty-one essentials for most snowy season hikes, especially those that take you into the mountains or foothills of the Cascades or Olympics. Items with an asterisk* should be included if weather or terrain conditions are such that you just might need them. Better to carry such items in and out without using them than to find yourself five miles along a trail and suddenly discovering you need something you don't have.

1. Extra food
2. Water treatment or filter
3. Extra clothing
4. Warm hat and mittens
5. Raincoat, rain pants
6. Gaiters
7. Sunglasses or snow goggles
8. Sunscreen and insect repellent
9. Map(s) of the area
10. Compass
11. Altimeter
12. Pocket knife
13. Fire starter
14. Matches in a waterproof container
15. Flashlight, with extra bulb and batteries
16. First aid kit
17. Instep crampons*
18. Ski pole (or pair)
19. Snowshoes*
20. Emergency shelter
21. Pack cover

Extra food

Extra food must be durable and well preserved. Think in terms of items that do not take lots of pack space and that require little to no cooking. Canned meats, jerky, dried fruits, nut mixes, granola, and food tubes filled with peanut butter are all good. Pilot biscuits (or Pilot crackers) are an excellent bread substitute and keep well after opening. Any such emergency foods should be used or replaced regularly.

Water treatment or filter

One can no longer drink from wilderness waters without great risk. Most pollution of surface waters is caused by humans, but even small animal feces contaminate snowfields and streams. Carry plenty of water in bottles filled at the kitchen sink, and also bring a reliable water filtration or treatment system, be it a stove for boiling water, iodine for treating it, or a good water filter with a pore size of four-tenths of a micron or smaller. Your biggest concern is the giardia cyst, a parasite that causes nausea, stomach cramps, headache, fever, and diarrhea, and that requires medical treatment. However, some waters closer to human activity may also carry bacterial and viral contaminants. Use good judgment and a reliable system.

Extra clothing

Extra clothing is just that, over and above what you have on. Both wear and carry wool and/or synthetics such as polypropylene and polyester, never cotton. (Cotton holds a lot of water and dries slowly, robbing your body of heat.) A set of polypropylene or other synthetic fibered long underwear weighs next to nothing but adds a lot of warmth, especially when exchanged for the damp set you might have on. A goosedown parka, again for its lightness-to-warmth ratio, makes great backup gear.

The key to comfort in cold weather is in not getting wet in the first place. Clothing should be planned and worn in layers. That warm down parka is great for lunching on top, but leave it in its stuff sack until then. Start hiking a little cold, and stop to peel layers before they become wet with perspiration. Keep your clothing dry for the higher-commitment zone. A 30-degree day with light wind at the trailhead may well become a 20-degree day with a 0-degree windchill factor on the summit.

Raincoat, rain pants

Dependable rain gear (which excludes the plastic cheapies) is a must in the Pacific Northwest, especially during the snowy season months. The greatest danger to anyone traveling in remote or mountainous areas is hypothermia—the loss of essential body heat. And the three things guaranteed to rob your body of heat are also the three most commonly encountered Northwest weather conditions from October to May: low temperatures, rain (even a drizzle), and wind. Guard against these religiously. Whether you prefer raingear made from a fully waterproof, nonbreathable fabric such as polyurethane-coated nylon, or from one of the more recently developed waterproof-breathable fabrics, carry it and wear it.

The rain coat will double as a windbreaker, and it should be fitted large enough to get all those layers under it without constricting movement. Buy two if necessary, for the one that looks and fits stylishly for wearing to the mall won't work in the woods. By all means, do not forget the rain pants. Without them, the legs become soaked and the feet will soon follow.

Gaiters

Even if you are wearing rain pants, gaiters help to keep sticks, gravel, and especially snow out of the boots. And please, put on the raingear and gaiters before getting wet. Mountain tragedies are always a combination of natural events and poor judgments. A cloudy day turns to freezing rain mixed with a wrong turn. Throw in poor map and compass skills, then top that off with a pair of cotton jeans and no raingear. What happens next often makes the five o'clock news.

Map(s), compass, and altimeter

It is strongly urged that those who venture into even moderately high country in winter give more than lip service and pack space to map and compass. The confidence in knowing how to use them extends as well to the pleasure of being able to spot and identify the numerous peaks, valleys, rivers, and far-off towns.

If your only skill with map and compass is being able to orient the map to true north, and from there to relate map features to terrain features, these abilities alone will add a respectable margin of safety.

In the vertical dimension, the altimeter adds a large measure of safety and satisfaction as well, and the instrument is easy to master. For one small example, when looking for a trail junction that the book or map shows to be at 2,600 feet, it is far easier to let the altimeter tell you when to really expect the turn. No more climbing to tree line before suspecting you may have missed the turn, which is now a thousand vertical feet back down the mountain.

In *Winter Hikes*, the reader will find many references to elevations and compass bearings, the latter mainly to aid in identifying terrain and other features from viewpoints. And although the trail descriptions contain references to both compass bearings and altimeter readings, the routes described in this book can be completed without dependence on either. These instruments are hedges on the margin of safety.

See Resources, at the end of the book, for additional readings on map, compass, and altimeter use.

What about GPS?

Global Positioning System receivers are hand-held, battery operated, electronic devices that average the return readings from three to six (or more) global satellites to tell you, in latitude and longitude (or other grid system), where you are. They will do so nearly anywhere on earth.

Make up your own mind about the device, but know this: A GPS receiver will give you your position and the degree reading (cardinal direction) of where you wish to go, but it will not show you the physical direction in which the route lies. Nor will it tell you if a cliff or a river or an avalanche track lies in the way. The GPS does not replace the functions of magnetic compass, altimeter, and topographic map.

In general terms, if you wander large bodies of water by boat, or travel untracked terrain, GPS could be a life saver. If your hiking is primarily on trails or at least along blazed routes, and especially if you are impatient with involved technology, GPS may not be for you. (See Resources, at the end of the book, for an excellent book on using GPS in wilderness navigation.)

Fire starter

Fire starter, or tinder, can be nearly any portable, flammable, nonbulky substance. A good fire starter can be made by cutting small pieces of corrugated cardboard, and then dipping them in melted paraffin. When needed, they burn long enough to dry out wet twigs to help in starting that all-important fire.

Flashlight

A flashlight will do for emergency lighting, but a headlamp is far superior. Lithium batteries are expensive, but last so much longer than either alkaline or rechargeable nicad batteries that there is good security in their purchase.

Instep crampons

Do not pack crampons. One should turn back long before the need for them is apparent. Instep crampons, however, are another matter. They are smaller, usually having only four points, and are much lighter and less bulky. They are also far less dangerous, so are worth packing. They can get you safely over a short icy traverse or across a mound of frozen avalanche debris blocking the trail.

Ski pole (or pair)
Ice axes are fine if carried for looks, but their more serious purposes put them in a category with crampons: too technical for winter hiking as defined by this book. They are also at the root of too many accidental injuries.

A ski pole, on the other hand, is great as a third leg for steep, gravelly trails and for previously trampled, now-frozen snow where balance is a problem. Perhaps carry a pair of them. The collapsible ones are handy, for they can be stowed when not needed.

Snowshoes
Snowshoes must be seriously considered for topping out on a few of the more lofty winter hikes. If you need them for more than a mile, or cannot tell where the trail is, the outing is no longer a "hike." Whether or not to take snowshoes will also depend on temperature and snowfall factors. Check ahead of time by calling the appropriate Forest Service office or other information center listed at the end of this book.

Emergency shelter
Carrying a sleeping bag or tent seems a bit much, but packing at least a large plastic leaf bag for the feet and legs, or perhaps a tube-tent, makes good sense. An emergency shelter of some sort, along with that parka and those well-traveled Pilot biscuits, could see you nicely through a bivouac.

Pack cover
The rain in the Pacific Northwest is not any wetter than anyone else's, but there is something persistent about it. Have a pack cover made, or at least take time to put spare clothing in plastic bags.

Planning for Safety
Create a Plan A and a Plan B for your trip, so you have something to fall back on if the weather changes or a trail is closed. Tell someone, in writing, where you will be. If you live alone or work at home, it could be days before you would be missed. Even if you are missed, authorities would have little to go on without knowing your intended destination. Deviate from the plan and you're on your own.

Solo hiking, especially in winter, is not a good idea, though many do it. Be aware of the risk factor, and be prepared to accept it.

Private Property

Each of us is a steward of any land we walk upon, but where privately owned lands are concerned, we must be keenly aware of having to earn and re-earn our welcome at all times. Beyond watching your own behavior, you can actively take up someone else's slack, for example, by picking up their litter and carrying it out.

Where passage over private property is not known to be a given, go out of your way to ask permission.

Choosing a Hike

The hikes in this guide have been selected for their all-around quality of experience as well as for their fit into the snowy season. Most are hikable all year. A few will have too much snow to make them passable from December through February; this is noted in the trail descriptions.

Many of the destinations are true summits, some are ridge walks, and a few are clifftops with great views. Others are favorite mountain lakes or exceptional lowland walks. They range from afternoon strolls to elevation gains of more than 3,000 vertical feet. In round-trip distances the outings go from under a mile to nearly fifteen miles.

Area Covered

The area covered by this book is roughly a thirty- to forty-mile-wide band on both sides of Puget Sound. It extends from northern King County to the Canadian border on the east side of Puget Sound, and from Mason to Clallam Counties and the Strait of Juan de Fuca on the west side of Puget Sound.

The Hike Outlines and Descriptions

At the beginning of each hike description is a brief outline summarizing the main characteristics of the route. Following are explanations of each category.

Ratings

The hikes are rated with the familiar one to five rating system, with one being low, and five being pretty terrific. In general, walks along forest road "trails," hikes with very long or strenuous routes, and those with inordinate difficulties such as very muddy or poorly maintained routes, lost a star. Those with combinations of the above lost two or three. Some, despite their bogs and blowdowns, were just plain groovy enough to rate a high five.

Distance

Distances for each hike have come from a variety of sources, including other guidebooks, trail signs, topographical maps (USGS, Green Trails, and others), as well as from calculations determined by actually hiking the trail.

Time

Walking times are based on the speed of a middle-of-the-pack hiker (about 2.25 miles an hour on an easy trail, 1.33 mph on moderately graded terrain, and 1 mph on a strenuous route). The walking times also take into account brief rest stops, some of the optional side trips, and of course, those extra moments spent in appreciation of a splendiferous view.

Once you've tried a few of the hikes in this book, and gauged your walking time against the ones given, you will probably conclude that Bob Mooers falls somewhere between a twenty-year-old peak bagger and an undermotivated octogenarian. And you will be right.

Starting elevation
The elevation at the trailhead.

High point
The highest point on the route, which frequently, but not always, is the destination. On some hikes, the highest point may be midway to the destination; on a couple (hikes into river gorges), the highest point is the starting elevation!

Trail type
The hikes in this book vary considerably, including ascents to the tops of peaks and cliffs; hikes along ridges and bluffs; and river, lake, and beach walks. Some are on forest roads, most are on trails; some are through forests to open views, others are along river gorges to waterfalls. The "Trail type" briefly sums up the main characteristics of the trail, the terrain, the surroundings, the type of route, and the destination. It is the hike at a glance.

Avalanche potential
Most of the hikes in this book have little or no avalanche danger. However, if even a potential of "slight" is noted in the hike description, do not venture onto the trail without first checking with the nearest Forest Service station regarding avalanche potential anywhere along the route (including the driving route). Changes in temperature or snowfall that have occurred in the last twenty-four hours can drastically increase avalanche potential. Be sure to get the most reliable and up-to-the-moment information.

Difficulty level
Each hike is assigned a difficulty level of easy, moderate, or strenuous. These judgments come from the author's own frame of reference, of course, but they are based on the following criteria: An "easy" level means the terrain is flat to sloping gently upward, perhaps to about 5 degrees. Strides will be normal with no more than slight additional effort in breathing. "Moderate" hikes have a sustained rise of 10 to 15 degrees, with strides two-thirds the length of normal and breathing rate approximately once every two steps. "Strenuous" indicates steep

grades of 25 to 35 degrees, necessitating strides half the length of normal, frequent pauses, and deep breaths at least every step. The difficulty rating also takes into consideration trail conditions and length.

Map(s)

This lists the recommended topographical map or maps to use for the hike. When topographic detail is important, I recommend USGS maps (in the 7.5-minute series), which provide the best and most readable topographical detail, important especially for less-frequented areas or poorly maintained routes. Green Trails maps are usually more up-to-date on both road and trail detail; they also have a smaller scale and therefore cover a wider area, so that at times, one Green Trails map will do in place of two USGS sheets. For most outings in the San Juan Islands, a good road map is the most useful to have. For hikes in the foothills and mountains, however, be sure to purchase (and know how to read) one of the recommended "topos." During the snowy season, when trails and weather conditions are unpredictable, accidentally wandering off the proper route could mean a long, cold night in the woods.

Route map

A small reproduction of a topographical map is provided for each hike, showing the route and main features. These are great visual aids, but are not intended to take the place of a good topographical map, such as the one(s) recommended at the beginning of each hike. Remember that the terrain is always going through changes. New logging roads are cut, trails are rerouted, and bridges wash out. Clear-cut logging operations wipe out long stretches of trail. Since guidebooks are months or even years in the making, and it is not possible to field-check all information at the last moment, all of them are slightly out-of-date even before they are printed. This sobering reality makes competency with map, compass, and altimeter all the more important.

Now let's do some winter hikes!

1 Sumas Mtn. Overlook

Distance:	9.0 miles round-trip
Time:	6.5 hours
Starting elevation:	490 feet
High point:	3,120 feet
Trail type:	Forest roads and trails to high views
Avalanche potential:	Slight
Difficulty level:	Strenuous
Map:	USGS Sumas Mountain and USGS Kendall (7.5' series)

The Hike

Sumas Mountain is unique among the foothills of western Washington. Close to the Canadian border, it is the last mountainous land mass in the northernmost contiguous United States. (The San Juan Islands and Olympic Mountains are considerably more to the south.) It is also the southern buttress of British Columbia's Fraser River Valley.

The Cheam Range in British Columbia, as seen from Sumas Mountain.

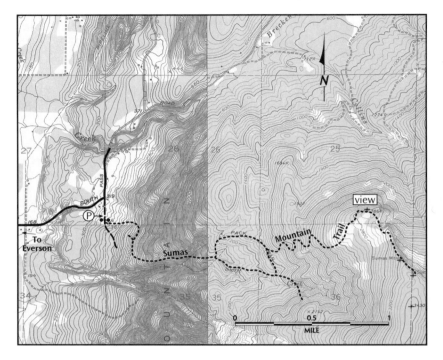

Getting There

Drive Interstate 5 to Bellingham Exit 256 (State Route 542). Go east 5.2 miles and turn left (north) on Everson–Goshen Road to its end at SR 544, East Pole Road. Follow SR 544 north and east into downtown Everson. Continue east to where SR 9 and a railroad track cross the route, virtually together.

Reset your vehicle's odometer at the double junction, but keep going east 2.4 miles, now on South Pass Road. Turn right (south) onto Sealand Road. At 2.9 miles from the track crossing, park on the right shoulder. (There is no formal parking area.) The correct site is slightly beyond the last visible house on the left and 25 yards before a small creek. The land across the creek is wooded and adorned with private property signs.

The Trail

The first 200 yards of trail, which goes left (east) along the south side of a barbed-wire fence, are very muddy summer or winter. However, the trail is in the only possible place, and the destination is worth the hassle.

When the fence turns left, go right (south) on much better trail. Turn left to join the remnants of an old mining road at the **0.5**-mile point. Soon the sounds of rushing Swift Creek arise from downslope to the right. After crossing the creek (and leaving most of the mud behind!), hear another branch of Swift Creek. Instead of crossing it, go left, leaving the mining road for steep trail. In just under a half mile, a broad, flat bench, 1,240 feet in elevation, brings brief relief from the steep gradient. A log cabin on the bench, usually uninhabited, is **1.4** miles from the trailhead.

Locate the trail again by continuing past the cabin along the same line as your approach. About a quarter mile from the building, the path crosses a usually dry creek bed. Just beyond, almost exactly where the flat bench abruptly ends, the trail forks. Go left, and very much up.

At **2.0** miles into the climb, avoid a right fork in the trail. Stay left, with the going quite steep, and shortly be rewarded by an oasis of mossy ledges at 1,780 feet. In summer, the moss here is laced with wild onion flowers—so many, in fact, that the onion scent lingers through the seasons. Follow the green carpet straight up to the forest. Shortly, another trail junction appears. Stay left.

At 2,700 feet, **3.6** miles from the starting point, the conifer forest thins out and the steep ascent moderates. At the same time, the trail enters a large stand of mixed alder, birch, and lots of native cherry.

At **4.0** miles the cherry thins and the evergreens reappear. A little farther along, glimpses of sky begin showing through the trees where the mountain suddenly falls away. Urge your muscles a quarter mile higher to an acre of open ledgy shoulder with drop-offs on its north and east sides. This is the Northern Overlook, 3,120 feet in elevation and **4.5** miles from the trailhead.

Drink in the magnificent panorama. It runs from towerlike Church Mountain in the east to Lummi Island in the west, with its Olympic Mountains backdrop. Most stunning is British Columbia's magnificent Cheam Range, whose row of massive peaks rises over Chiliwack in the northeast at a general bearing of 68 degrees.

The trail continues for 0.8 mile to the summit of Sumas Mountain. The summit is wooded and viewless, but the half mile above the overlook follows the precipitous rim of what appears to be a glacial cirque. This portion is very much worth the extra effort.

2 Gunsight Notch

Distance:	6.3 miles round-trip
Time:	4 hours
Starting elevation:	90 feet
High point:	1,435 feet
Trail type:	Forest roads and trails to high, sandstone cliffs
Avalanche potential:	None
Difficulty level:	Easy to moderate; occasionally strenuous
Map:	USGS Bellingham South (7.5' series)

A unique trail marker.

The Hike

The word "gunsight" comes easily to mind when viewing this notch from Interstate 5. Heading south from Bellingham, look up as you approach Exit 252 (State Route 11/Chuckanut Drive) and there it is, right over the freeway, a deep notch in a rugged ridge parallel to Chuckanut Ridge.

There are lots of old roads and trails on Chuckanut Mountain, and at press time a much-needed plan was in the works for systematically signing and maintaining them. When you take this hike, you may find a few signs with names other than those described here.

Getting There

Drive I-5 to Exit 252, the northern end of SR 11. Follow it west 1.3 miles to a traffic light. SR 11 turns left (south). Cross a bridge to a five-way intersection. Bear left again, onto Chuckanut Drive. At 2.6 miles from I-5 (milepost 18.5) and immediately before reaching California Street on the left, turn left and down into the parking area for Teddy Bear Cove and the Interurban Trail. (In the future the signage will likely read "North Chuckanut Mountain Trailhead.")

The Trail

The first part of the trail is a connector, which leads out of the parking area on its south side and rises to join the Interurban Trail in **0.2** mile. Turn left (northeast) on the Interurban. On the way, linger to hear the magic of a pleasant falls in California Creek. Steeply down to the left is Chuckanut Creek.

At the **0.5**-mile point, turn right (east) and climb moderately upward on a trail marked for Lost Lake. At **1.0** mile, the trail flattens out and joins a forest road a few hundred feet behind an old log home. The road is an extension of California Street. Turn left (southeast) and at **1.2** miles reach a junction.

The right fork here, the North Lost Lake Trail, will serve as your return route from Chuckanut Ridge. For now, go straight (southeast) on the California Street Extension, now signed Pine and Cedar Lakes. At **1.7** miles reach a three-way intersection. Turn right, leaving the California Street Extension/Pine and Cedar Lakes Trail and take the old road up into Gunsight Notch. It starts south but swings to the west, contouring steep slopes.

At 900 feet, and looking southwest beyond the road, see sandstone cliffs. These form the west wall of the notch.

The Salal Crossover Trail is not far above you. The road steepens and climbs parallel to the wall. Keep a sharp watch for an opening in the young trees where the trail goes right. (At **2.1** miles and 940 feet elevation lies a huge boulder 5 feet from the right side of the road and about 10 feet beyond the start of the crossover trail. The road is still moderately steep prior to and shortly beyond this junction, but if you reach the place where it levels out to a gentle rise, you have passed the opening, though not by very much.)

Three stone steps go up and over a mound, then dense, very dark forest at the base of the wall on your left engulfs the path. With some interesting ducking and clutching, you are soon above the notch.

The trail drops slightly, briefly paralleling the wall downward through lush salal before turning sharply left into mature forest. (In the future, a new link may lead from this sharp turn back to the notch road.) In another half mile, **2.5** miles from the trailhead, the crossover trail intersects North Lost Lake Trail. Turn right (northwest) but only for 75 yards or so, then look for another trail on the left.

The North Chuckanut Link Trail is a rough crossover that joins the high trail along Chuckanut Ridge in a tenth of a mile. Find it, then drop down an embankment to slosh across a small stream.

Join the Chuckanut Ridge Trail at **2.7** miles, and turn left (south). Note the very distinctively twisted tree near the intersection. It is better than a store-bought sign in marking the correct turn on the way down.

You are now in mountain bike country, so listen and be ready to assert your presence. The trail soon begins to climb southeast, and since Chuckanut Ridge is higher than most of the surrounding terrain, the views begin to assert *their* presence as well. In no time, sandstone balconies have you looking across and down at the tips of 175-foot firs.

The first few open ledges have more northerly exposures than those higher up. Look due north to British Columbia's Golden Ears, twin peaks towering over all of their neighbors. In the foreground is the green oasis of Sehome Hill. Western Washington University sprawls along Sehome's lower western edge. The less-defined high mountains to the far left are those of the Coast Range as far north as Whistler, British Columbia.

Continue up. The high point of this northern end of Chuckanut Mountain is 1,435 feet. It is **3.3** miles into the hike and is the turnaround point for the day. Chuckanut Ridge Trail (Hike 3) goes all the way to Cyrus Gates Overlook, a 6.6-mile round-trip from here.

Mount Baker, visible from any point of the rim, is big and beautiful, and North and South Twin Sisters are standouts in white relief to Baker's south. Lookout Mountain's two nearly identical summits are next in line, both with communications equipment on their tops.

Distant as these heights may seem, the rush of traffic on I-5 will call you down eventually. Return via North Chuckanut Link by turning right at the oddly bent tree. Turn left (northwest) on North Lost Lake Trail, and close the loop at the California Street Extension in slightly more than a mile. From there, return the way you came.

3 Chuckanut Ridge Trail

Distance:	7.0 miles round-trip
Time:	4.5 hours
Starting elevations:	1,710 feet or 1,250 feet
High point:	1,710 feet
Trail type:	Ridge walk with forest on one side, escarpment on the other
Avalanche potential:	None
Difficulty level:	Easy to moderate
Map:	USGS Bellingham South (7.5' series)

The Hike

The easy way to do this ridge walk is to drive to Cyrus Gates Overlook, an 1,800-foot viewpoint on Chuckanut Ridge, and start there, but that limits you to only its fine views to the east. Fortunately, a neat little loop alternative provides some equally fine views out over the island kingdom.

Getting There

From the south, take Interstate 5 Exit 231 in Burlington and drive north on State Route 11 to Highline Road. Take a right there (east) exactly at milepost 16. From the north, take I-5 Exit 252, the northern end of SR 11, and follow it 6.9 miles south to MP 16. Turn left (east) on Highline Road. Highline very quickly becomes Cleator Road.

Reset your odometer as you turn off SR 11. At 2.1 miles, 1,250 feet elevation, look for a trail, actually an overgrown forest road on the left (north). The best way to spot it is to look for double orange blazes on a 10- to 12-inch-thick cedar on the right (south) side of the road. Park there.

The Trail

Walk northward and gently up. At **0.7** mile the trees thin and an obvious 50-foot side path leads left (west) to a picture-perfect view over the northern sound. Lummi Island dominates the view, but gaze past it to Mount Constitution on Orcas Island. If the day is clear, there is no problem picking out the snowcapped peaks on Vancouver Island, 75 to 100 miles in the distance.

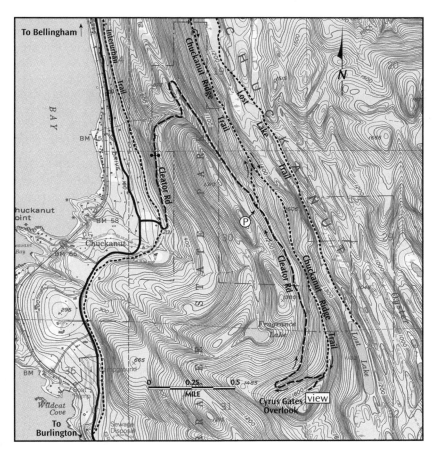

Back on the main route, it is slightly more than a quarter mile to a T junction with the Chuckanut Ridge Trail at the **1.0**-mile point. This is also the 1,350-foot low point of the ridge.

Go left (north) for a quarter to a half mile and start wowing over the views again. How far you walk is your choice, but past a half mile the views will be over. Spectacular images of Mount Baker dominate the eastern skyline from numerous ledgy lookouts. To Baker's right are the very symmetrical cones of the North and South Twin Sisters. To their right, and hiding the rest of the rugged Twin Sisters Range, is another set of twins, the two summits of Lookout Mountain. Each wears a crown of communications towers.

Toward the end, just before the trail starts sharply downward, Chuckanut Ridge veers slightly northwest, permitting wider horizons to the north. One can see a slice of Bellingham Bay and most of the city, all backdropped by the mountains of British Columbia. Due north, and right over I-5, are the twin spires of Golden Ears Mountain.

Stare long enough and you risk seeing double. There in the northeast is Sumas Mountain, at 24 degrees, but what is that peak at 36 degrees? It's Sumas Mountain, of course. One is in the United States (Hike 1), the other in Canada, and right between them you look deep into the Fraser River Canyon, British Columbia's gateway to its interior.

When at last you can tear yourself away, it's up and down the scenic ridge bumps as you head south, bypassing the West Spur Chuckanut Ridge Trail you came up on, for 3.3 miles back to Cleator Road. At **5.3** miles so far, an easy walk downhill completes the **7.0**-mile loop at the trailhead.

4 Lookout Mountain

Distance:	11.0 miles round-trip
Time:	6 hours
Starting elevation:	630 feet
High point:	2,677 feet
Trail type:	Gated forest road to summit
Avalanche potential:	None
Difficulty level:	Balance of easy, moderate, and strenuous
Map:	USGS Lake Whatcom (7.5' series)

The Hike

Considering that the northern end of Lookout Mountain is within Bellingham's city limits, the far-reaching views from its summit are a grand surprise. The mountain, sporting two competing summits with a single foot difference in elevation, rises from Lakeway Drive in the north and runs for nearly 8 air miles before bowing at the dainty foot of splendid little Alger Alp (Hike 23).

Parking and access for the summit route are on private property in the resident-owned community of Sudden Valley. Let us continue to earn their good will.

Getting There

From the south, take Interstate 5 Exit 240, Alger, and drive east 0.8 mile to cross Old Pacific Highway at the Alger Bar and Grill. In 6.8 miles, go left at a Y. At 8.7 miles from I-5, with Sudden Valley in sight around a bend, turn left (west) onto Lake Louise Road for an additional half mile to Sudden Valley's Gate 5. Turn left (west) through the gate. Shortly up the hill, where the road splits, follow it to the right on Tumbling Water Drive and take the second left onto Little Palomino Place. Park there, 9.4 miles from I-5, well away from the only house on the street.

From the north, take I-5 Exit 253, Lakeway Drive, and go east. The drive changes name several times, but you simply opt for the main flow of traffic. Shortly, see Lake Whatcom, and halfway down a steep hill, at 3.5 miles from I-5, turn right (west) onto Austin Street. After a stop sign, go straight up the hill.

At 7.5 miles from I-5, turn right through Sudden Valley Gate 5. Follow the directions given above to park and start the walk.

The Trail

From Little Palomino Place, walk north along a road remnant, paved as far as a set of big boulders, and join Lookout Mountain Road in about **0.1** mile. Turn left and rise moderately to a Y at **0.6** mile. Take the left branch and parallel the playfully resounding waters of the west fork of Austin Creek. When the road crosses the creek, the easy part is over for a while. It is a bit over 2.5 miles from the first Y to a second one, and half the distance (still to come) is nearly flat while the other half is steep. Keep thinking "views."

The next Y is at the **3.2**-mile point, identified by Puget Sound Energy power boxes. Here the north summit route goes right. (If you simply cannot leave such things alone, a left here leads to the south summit with its tiny peek down into Lake Samish.) Steep is not over yet, but the route is mostly moderate to gentle from here, and views are less than a mile away.

The road tops the main ridge and a low saddle at **4.0** miles and 2,250 feet. Fine views extend to the west. This is also a good turnaround spot if your energy is flagging. Look down into Lake Samish with Blanchard Mountain and the Oyster Dome directly behind the lake. Then, with the gush of new motivation, be on your way to the top. The mere 1.5 miles to go exert a powerful antigravity influence, and the vistas east begin along the way.

Views from Lookout's summit are had from three stances. Views east and south are best from the road about a half mile before reaching the top. Mount Baker is a can't-miss, but do not forget the entire burnished brown profile of the Twin Sisters Range, which runs all the way to Lyman and Hamilton on the North Cascades Highway.

On the summit, **5.5** miles from Little Palomino Place, trees block views north and to most of the southeast, but the magnificent sweep of lands and seas to the west is crimped only slightly by one of the steel gendarmes. With a properly oriented map you can pick out dozens of misty isles and even spot some of the larger peaks of the Olympic Mountains. Follow the islands all the way to Canada's Vancouver Island. And there's no stopping here, oh no!

About 0.3 mile back down the road, go right (northwest) on a wide, rough cat track for 0.2 mile to a log landing on the brink of forever. Fill in all of the

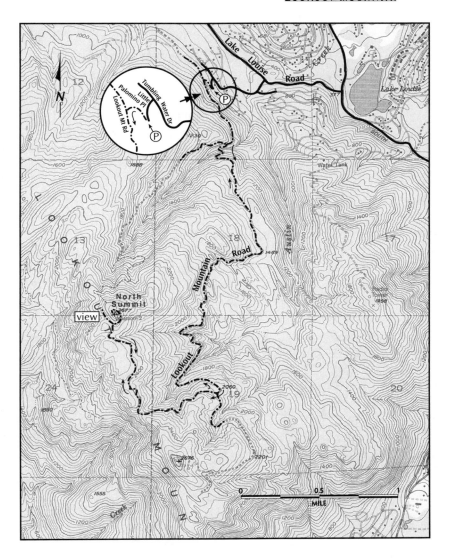

gaps with a miles-wide look over the north sound and half of Whatcom County. Beyond the residences, see the prairie farmlands smooth the way far north to the Fraser River and British Columbia's mountain kingdom.

5 Doing the Nooksack

Distance:	2.4 miles total
Time:	2 hours
Starting elevation:	1,000 feet
High point:	1,200 feet
Trail type:	River walk through forest
Avalanche potential:	None
Difficulty level:	Easy
Map:	Green Trails Mount Baker No. 13

The Hike

This hike is a double feature: a charming walk along the beautiful North Fork Nooksack River followed by a short drive to a tour of thundering Nooksack Falls a few miles upstream. The wild North Fork is headwatered in precipitous

Rafters "doing the Nooksack" below Horseshoe Bend.

Nooksack Cirque on Mount Shuksan's northeast side. It does not stop its wild celebration until well below the community of Glacier.

Getting There

Take Interstate 5 Exit 256 in Bellingham and drive east on State Route 542. Pass through Glacier to a Nooksack crossing at milepost 35.5. Cross the bridge and park on the right.

The Trail

The trail gets right down to the river and never wanders far above or away from its throaty presence. It pushes through the splendor of moss-draped vine maple amid mature firs. The forest floor is dressed in just the right accents of fern, salal, and beard lichen.

Everybody's favorite stopping place is at **0.5** mile. A wooden bench sits on a flat slab next to the churning river. Something cataclysmic has happened here, for big boulders litter the riverbed as if tossed by a hand larger than life. Water piles up against them, then surges between and around as it hurries down toward more of the same, certainly, but also toward infinite variations.

A steepening riverbank forces a brief detour on good trail at **0.7** mile. The route rises about a hundred vertical feet, then passes beneath light-duty power lines at the top. It then turns right onto an old road. In 200 feet the trail picks up once more and goes right.

At **0.9** mile, a slide has wiped out a section of trail on a steep traverse. Intrepid souls have kicked some pretty good steps up the slope and around the impasse, but more have turned back at this point than have forged ahead. Beyond the slide, the lack of maintenance by footsteps becomes more and more apparent. Blowdowns and washouts become tedious, especially with no clear-cut destination in mind. When you have reached your own limit, turn around and enjoy it all again going back.

To see Nooksack Falls, return to the highway, drive east to MP 40.6, and turn right on Wells Creek Road, which at its beginning is a one-lane pothole with turnouts. Fortunately, it is only 0.5 mile to a parking area on the left just before a bridge above the falls.

Follow people trails or a chain-link fence a short distance to see the awesome twin-tongued drop of 170 feet. Wells Creek enters the river at the base of the precipice, then, strangely, appears to head slightly upstream as if irresistibly drawn to the fall's plunge pool.

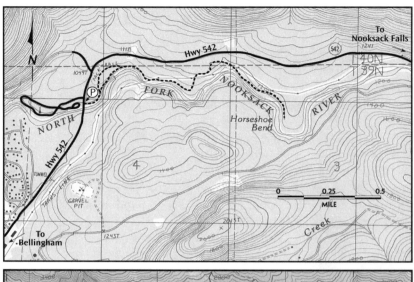

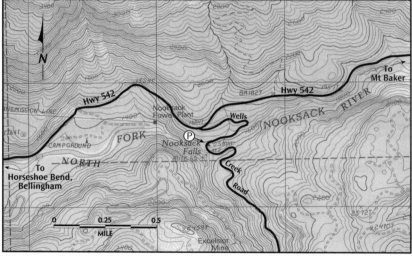

Do not leave without taking an appreciative look at the huge wooden penstock in the trees along the north side of the parking area. It is made of wooden planks, tapered and banded together like an oak barrel. Though it sports a leak or two, and is encrusted with moss, the penstock has been in continuous use for a lot of years.

6 Bowman Mountain

🥾🥾

Distance:	12.5 miles round-trip
Time:	6.75 hours
Starting elevation:	650 feet
High point:	3,356 feet
Trail type:	Forest roads to an old lookout site
Avalanche potential:	Slight
Difficulty level:	Moderate to strenuous
Maps:	USGS Acme, Cavanaugh Creek, and Canyon Lake (7.5' series)

The Hike

Never heard of Bowman Mountain? Why would you? But, of the four approaches to the magnificent Twin Sisters Range, two of them go over Bowman, and the mountain's all-but-forgotten lookout site has an upstairs-window view of the impressive yard next door, that of Mount Baker.

A note of caution: Bowman Mountain Lookout Site is only a 3,300-footer, but it sits just 10 air miles from Mount Baker, a definite weather maker. This hike calls for careful planning when attempted in the winter months. Pick a low snow year, or perhaps plan Bowman for April or May.

The focus of this hike is an old lookout site at the extreme northern end of the mountain. The final half mile is on a brushy, alder-choked, log road remnant. The other 5.75 miles of road, however, comprise the interstate of gravel highways, and as such are wide open for mountain bikes.

Getting There

Drive State Route 9 to Acme. Immediately north of town, on the north bank of the south fork of the Nooksack River, turn east on Mosquito Lake Road. At 4.2 miles from SR 9, look for address number 2519 on the left (west) and a gated gravel road on the right (east). Park without blocking the gate.

The Trail

Walk east from the gate and proceed to Musto Marsh at **1.7** miles. Ignore right turns immediately before and after the marsh. At **2.2** miles (1,140 feet)

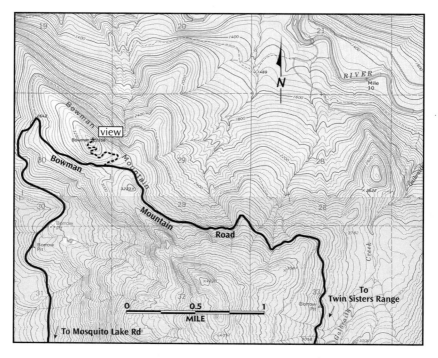

go right at a fork (painted arrow on a tree). Ignore a right turn at **2.4** miles. At **2.6** miles, go right at a Y as the road steepens. At 1,660 feet you will see a painted "3.0" on a tree, the last in a series of mileage postings.

Ignore a right turn at a gravel pit at **3.6** miles (2,060 feet). By 2,100 feet the road travels through a recent clear-cut and climbs along the edge of steep slopes. Views are great down the SR 9 valley and northward to a small slice of prairie at Everson.

At **4.8** miles (2,640 feet) northward progression ends abruptly as the road switchbacks sharply southeast, then east, getting steeper.

Soon, a critical turn appears: When the road levels out to a paltry bare incline, look hard for an overgrown spur road left, **5.5** miles (3,020 feet). It takes off at a low angle, with a grass-covered but telltale berm at the start.

Though brushy, the way up is easily found except for one place. About ten minutes upward, a tiny but distinctive clearing is reached. With a bit of looking around, not one but two ancient left-trending road segments can be found. The one you want is the inside or more left of the two, the one that climbs. Toward the summit the track becomes more open, then suddenly, there the summit is. Celebrate by hugging one of the four sawed-off former lookout supports.

Views are affected by a few treetops, but are, oh, so dramatic. The base of North Twin Sister (6,570 feet) is barely 4 road miles away. Pivot your eyes leftward and follow the Black Buttes right up to the 10,778th and final foot of ice-clad Mount Baker. Below your location lies the valley of the Middle Fork Nooksack River. It drains much of Baker's southwest quadrant.

7 | Bear Mountain

Distance:	5.6 miles round-trip
Time:	4.5 hours
Starting elevation:	2,360 feet
High point:	4,200 feet
Trail type:	Gated forest roads and ridge walk
Avalanche potential:	Slight
Difficulty level:	Moderate to partly strenuous
Maps:	USGS Lyman, Hamilton, Cavanaugh Creek, and Twin Sisters Mountain (7.5' series)

The Hike

Crown Pacific builds good logging roads for the purpose (it thinks) of harvesting wood fiber, but you know better. One of its roads, at least, is there to enhance your view of some pretty distinctive geology. The road to the top of Bear Mountain is a veritable grandstand from which to watch the parade of jagged peaks in the Twin Sisters Range. The Twins constitute the largest

A view of the Twin Sisters Range from Bear Mountain.

known contiguous mass of olivine bedrock in the Western world, and the light green material is quarried and sold widely as building stone.

Getting There

Drive State Route 20 from Interstate 5 Exit 230 in Burlington, and go east to the Hamilton turnoff at milepost 77.4. Turn left. Follow the road 0.7 mile. Immediately after it crosses signed Muddy Creek, it comes to an unsigned intersection. Turn right (north) for 0.3 mile, and stop for an entry permit at the Crown Pacific Guard Station, open 6 a.m. to 10 p.m. daily.

Reset your odometer and drive on. This is Main Line Road, or Road 100. At 5.9 miles stay right at a Y. Past a huge flattened area of gravel the road splits.

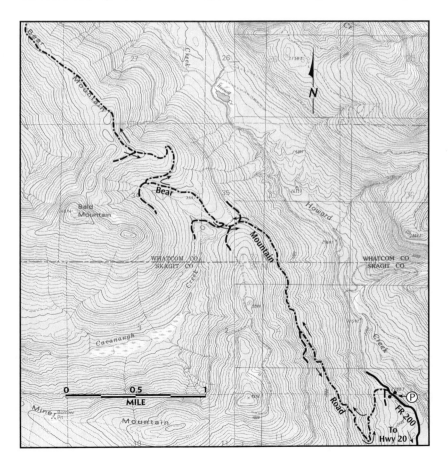

Bear right (east) again. At 9.2 miles from the guard station, a gated road goes right. Stay left, now signed as Forest Road 200. In a couple hundred yards, cross the South Fork Nooksack River and start climbing. Due to a dwindling local elk herd, the road is gated at the 13.0-mile mark. Park.

The Trail

Immediately inside the gate, the road splits three ways. Take the center choice and start upward. Within minutes, views of the Twins begin off the right side of the road and just keep getting better.

The climb is somewhat steep for just shy of a mile. Two delightful, trickle-and-chute waterfalls lie about 50 feet apart at the 3,000-foot level, and from there the grade slacks off to moderate. At the **0.9**-mile mark (3,160 feet), the route joins another road on a sharp angle. Go right (northwest).

At **1.6** miles (3,500 feet) is the first of three road junctions in quick succession. Take a left at the first one. Choose the right (northwest) fork at the second Y, then go right at the third fork. Incidentally, there are great views from the first of the three intersections.

At **2.0** miles, ignore a road leading left off a bulbous swing of the main gravel road. Follow the rounded turn right (easterly) and up. Do not watch only the rhythm of your feet in this uppity quarter-mile slow sprint. Look off to the south as well, for there sits the mound of ice, rock, and snow called Glacier Peak as well as the distinctive horn of Whitechuck Mountain. After the south view and the breather of a flat section that follows, the road makes another big bend, this time back to the south from where it climbs again. Past there, you only need to avoid one more side road left (southwest).

Top the ridge and the whole reason for climbing here spreads to the east. Across the valley, bathed in pastel brown, lies the intriguing Twin Sisters Range. Prominent among the array of peaks are North and South Twin Sisters (6,570 feet and 6,930 feet) at the north end of the ridge. The pointy little summit to the right of South Sister is named Skookum, and it is Skookum Creek and Falls you both see and hear two-thirds of the way downrange from north to south. The blocky knob south of Skookum Peak, projecting more westerly than most in the line, is Hayden, followed by Little Sister and Cinderella and then a drop-off to tiny Boot Lake and Boot Lake Pass. Look south from there to Saddle Slab Peak, Shirley Peak, then Trisolace, Barbara, and Nancy. The final upthrust of rock, a 5,500-footer, has not been dignified with a name, though it, too, has been climbed.

You will be long gone from Bear Mountain before this memory fades.

8 East Bank Trail

Distance:	3.8 miles round-trip
Time:	3 hours
Starting elevation:	980 feet
High point:	980 feet (lake level approximately 750 feet)
Trail type:	Gently downward through forest to Baker Lake
Avalanche potential:	None
Difficulty level:	Easy to moderate
Maps:	USGS Welker Peak (7.5' series) or Green Trails Lake Shannon No. 46

Restful forests along the East Bank Trail.

The Hike

If a walk in a forest is balm for weary minds, the East Bank Trail at Baker Lake has to be in the running for a full-blown cure. The trail is lined with both old growth and cut-over land, but time and rich growing conditions have so healed the forest that the only obvious scars are the occasional big stumps.

Getting There

Drive east on State Route 20 from Interstate 5 Exit 230 in Burlington. At milepost 82.4, turn left (north) onto Baker Lake Road. Reset your odometer. Turn right (east) on Baker Dam Road at the 13.8-mile mark. Drive across the one-lane top of the dam a mile and a half later. At 16.1 miles, go left and upward on a road signed for Watson Lakes. At 16.9 miles from SR 20, park on the left at the trailhead.

The Trail

It is not long before the tall ones begin, bringing with them the sound and presence of a cathedral when no one else is there. The trail, contouring a steep-sided ridge, soon begins to snake in and out of little ravines. Small bridges are welcome and frequent.

At about **1.0** mile, the trail begins to steepen its glide. As the trail curls into a large ravine, hear the rushing, tumbling waters of Anderson Creek at **1.4** miles. You will be glad for the sturdy bridge to carry you to the opposite bank, but the old one, built of 20-inch-thick logs and cabled in place 10 feet above normal high water, was swept away by the flood nobody could plan for.

The crossing of Anderson Creek is close to the lakeshore. There are nice campsites at the mouth of the creek, but the number of accommodations depends on the height of the manipulated lake level.

On the north bank of the creek begins the only real ascending to be done on the way "down," but it is neither high to climb nor far to go. At **1.7** miles turn left (west) at a junction. Just **1.9** miles from Watson Lake Road the trail ends at the lake with a pretty view of Mount Baker off the end of a point.

9 Baker River Trail

Distance:	5.2 miles round-trip
Time:	3.5 hours
Starting elevation:	800 feet
High point:	1,040 feet
Trail type:	Through forest and along the river
Avalanche potential:	Slight to none
Difficulty level:	Easy
Maps:	Green Trails Mount Shuksan No. 14

The Hike

For being so close to the heart of the North Cascades, Baker River Trail is a dependable snowy-season hike. The trail leads past a river that at times can be a raging torrent, then it leaves the river for the life-filled quietude of a

Baker River seems always ready to adjust its banks—the trail is no obstacle.

huge beaver marsh. The trail ends at the unbridged tributary of Sulphide Creek in the shadow of the remote Picket Range.

Getting There

From Burlington, drive east on State Route 20 to milepost 82.4 and turn left on Baker Lake Road. Drive 26.2 miles, 20.0 of them paved, to the end of the

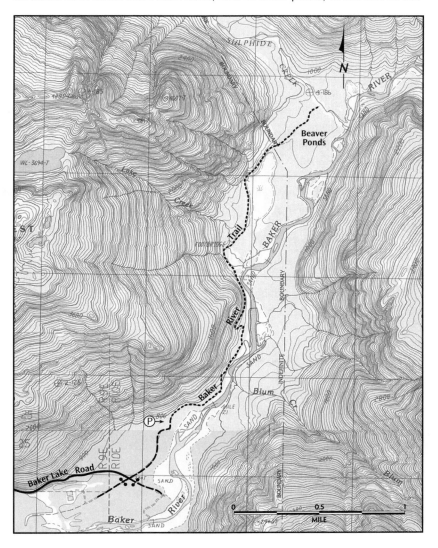

road. Park in a large graveled area. The trail, actually an old road for the first 0.2 mile, is straight ahead.

The Trail

The walking begins on an abandoned remnant of the access road. At **0.2** mile it ends where the river has chewed it off. Go left at the brink into a green land of moss-carpeted boulders and lichen-draped trees. Soon the route reaches the swishing river.

At **0.3** mile are the steel and concrete beginnings of what is shaping up to become a suspension bridge. A recent extension of the East Bank Trail (Hike 8) brings that route all the way up the east shore of Baker Lake and Baker River to this point on the other side, a distance of 14.0 miles. A bridge link with the Baker River Trail makes a good two- or three-day backpack.

Just beyond the bridge site, undercutting by floodwater has collapsed the bank. With a few gymnastic movements, you will be over that hump. Rerouting will likely occur soon, since this trail is so popular.

Back on the trail, the track is in and out from restful forest to restive river. For a trail with so little apparent elevation gain, it seems to rise and fall a lot, 50 to 100 feet at a time, but the mix of up and down is pleasant. At **1.6** miles from the trailhead the beaver marsh begins. The area is so big that it takes nearly a quarter mile to pass it all, and it is wider than you can see. The trail then leaves the marshes and Baker River behind to enter peaceful forest.

Not far beyond the beaver digs, you come to a talus pile and slide-alder clearing. Look up and left (about 60 degrees) and see the great gash in the northern wall of the Baker River Valley, a huge ravine cut by wild Sulphide Creek, not far from here.

At **2.6** miles Sulphide Creek blocks any reasonable thought of continuing up the Baker River. To all except those bent on real bushwhacking to reach remote mountains, this is the end of the trail.

Go upstream to the left along the near bank of the rushing creek. There is no trail, but easy brush dodging for 200 to 300 feet is enough to reach a glimpse of 7,500-foot Jagged Ridge. Sulphide Creek drains a huge cirque on Mount Shuksan's southeast side, then most of Jagged Ridge plus Mount Seahpo as well. It is called a creek but looks for all the world like it could have been dubbed the North Fork Baker River.

10 Doing the Skagit

Distances:	2.5 to 5.0 miles total
Times:	Up to 5 hours
Starting elevation:	Diablo Dam powerhouse, 896 feet
High point:	1,300 feet
Trail types:	Various: riverine forest to lake environment
Avalanche potential:	Slight
Difficulty level:	Easy to moderate to a touch of strenuous
Maps:	USGS Diablo Dam and USGS Mount Triumph (7.5' series)

Verdant arches shelter a river trail.

The Hike

This is a day for superlatives. Stroll to giant cedars, walk to a waterfall, ogle 7,000-foot peaks, hike up a dam, ride a diagonal rail platform (for free), eat buffalo burgers (not free), cross the Skagit on footbridges, drive over a dam, view a glittering lake—but wait: You won't actually hike up the dam, and doing the diagonal thing, which is either a steep railroad or a confused elevator, depends on the season.

Getting There

Drive east on State Route 20 from Interstate 5 Exit 230 in Burlington. (The buffalo burgers are found at the Buffalo Run restaurant in Marblemount.) First stop is the North Cascades Visitors Center at milepost 119.9 in Newhalem.

The Trails

Turn right (south) at MP 119.9, crossing the Skagit on a single-lane bridge. Drive to the visitors center, park, and walk behind the building on its left side. A short stroll leads to a small overlook, but one with a big view. Framed between the valley walls of Goodell Creek is a picture-perfect shot of 8,151-foot Mount Terror. (The visitors center has some excellent displays, too.)

Back on the highway, drive only 0.7 mile and turn right (south) in the center of town at a flashing crosswalk signal. Park at the end of the block to walk the Trail of the Cedars, which begins with a sturdy suspension bridge over the Skagit and makes a 0.7-mile loop. It is easy walking studded with awesome old-growth western red cedars. Return to your car or leave it where it is, and walk to the next surprise, a tour of Ladder Creek Falls.

Just 0.2 mile east along SR 20 is the Gorge Powerhouse, on the right, and plenty of parking. Across the river, Ladder Creek joins the Skagit, leaping and gushing its anguish, presumably at having to give up its freedom. City Light has constructed walks and stairways up along the defile.

There are two bridges here, one for service vehicles and one for pedestrians. The Ladder Creek Loop Trail starts at the footbridge at the south end of the parking area. The loop can be done in 20 minutes, but it is not difficult at all to expend an hour absorbing its magic.

Now drive 6.0 miles up the scenic gorge to another City Light town called Diablo. On the way, stop at Gorge Creek Falls, right on the highway at MP 123.4. The left turn for Diablo is at MP 126. Drive 0.7 mile to a one-way bridge over Stetatle Creek, then go right at a Y. This will take you past the

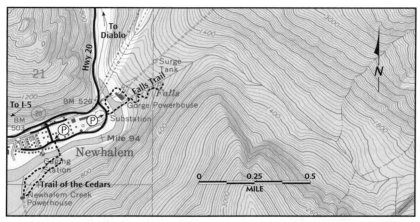

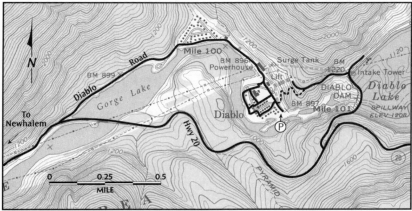

Diablo powerhouse, then the community hall and the Incline Railway office. Keep going, but on the left just beyond the impressive railway-elevator diagonal, park near a sign announcing the Diablo Dam Trail. (The trailhead is a total of 1.4 miles from SR 20.) Park away from the "Busses Only" signs, then look hard at the wall of rock before you.

Before Diablo Dam and then Ross Dam were built, there was no road much beyond Newhalem. One was forced as far as the Diablo townsite, but it was all gorge and the rising bedrock of Sourdough Mountain from there. An incline, or funicular railway, was constructed to lift men, equipment, and materials to construction sites. It is still a primary means of transport upriver, and to this day there is no road to Ross Dam. Moving up the side of the mountain on the lift's huge platform provides a rush of its own: Like a miniversion of our expanding universe, valley and mountain scenes burgeon in time-lapse fashion as you rise.

The railway is no substitute for walking the trail up the same wall of rock. In places it is more carved than built. At **0.2** mile, a switchback does its thing almost beneath the tracks of the incline, then leads away and to an overlook of the valley. From the ledge, snowcapped giants loom at the head of Stetattle Creek Valley. The largest is 7,266-foot Elephant Butte. Looking south, find colossal Colonial Peak (169 degrees and 7,774 feet up). Its impressive right-hand neighbor, no slouch at 7,182 feet, is aptly named Pyramid Peak.

Climbing higher, the shoulder of Sourdough pushes southward, jamming the Skagit between walls more than 400 feet high. Look steeply downward, but watch your footing. After another 0.4 mile, the trail reaches a blacktop roadway at lake level (1,220 feet). What is now road was conventional railroad track in the building days. Left goes to the upper station of the Incline Railway, right leads to Diablo Lake and Dam in a stretched tenth of a mile, **0.5** mile total from parking.

Walk the dam and the lakeshore. From the dam, it is 2.2 miles additional round-trip to a gate at road's end on the north shore of Diablo Lake. (It is this choice, and walking the dam, that total the 2.5- to 5.0-mile spread in the opening stats.)

The big mountain (110 degrees from the north buttress of the dam) is Ruby. Ruby-the-Creek figures into the colorful history of the North Cascades, for gold was discovered there in the 1890s. Predictably, it caused the usual boom-and-bust reaction.

If you don't have a nice day doing the Skagit, it's because you went some-place else for the burgers.

11 Diablo Lake Trail

Distance:	5.4 miles round-trip
Time:	4.5 hours
Starting elevation:	1,240 feet
High point:	2,140 feet
Trail type:	Walk through forest to the rim of Skagit River Canyon
Avalanche potential:	Cautionary
Difficulty level:	Moderate
Map:	Green Trails Diablo Dam No. 48

The Skagit River Gorge, seen from the Diablo Lake Trail.

The Hike

The Diablo experience is vintage North Cascades hiking at its earth, water, and bedrock finest. It is a heart-slamming passage from a high mountain dam, and the emerald waters of the lake it holds in check, to and across the face of the river-carved gorge that gives it all meaning.

Getting There

Drive State Route 20, the North Cascades Highway, through Marblemount and Newhalem, then past the turn-off to the Seattle City Light town of Diablo. At milepost 127.5 turn left (north) on Diablo Dam Access Road. Reach the far side of the dam in 0.5 mile and turn right. Drive east along the lakeshore to a parking area and gate (signed Diablo Lake Resort) at 1.6 miles from SR 20. The trailhead leads up along Sourdough Creek, right out of the large graveled parking site.

The Trail

The trail starts in hardwoods to the right of the creek, a waterway that has the look of a fearsome place to be in high water. At **0.3** mile the trail intersects an old road and runs downhill to the right with it for 50 feet. Here, as elsewhere, the path is well signed. It drops to cross two creeks, then begins to climb, paralleling the second stream for a while.

Immediately away from the water the silence swoops in, bearing with it the quiet mystery of the forest. It will likely bring you back again and again, but no one can ever fathom its composition, let alone give it voice.

At **1.5** miles (1,800 feet), an opening in the trees permits the first views down on Diablo Lake. This is close to where the free-flowing Skagit River emerges from its steep-walled canyon. Across the chasm is wonderfully alpine Colonial Peak, strung with spider webs of white. The mountain west of Colonial is Pyramid Peak.

Above the viewpoint, the route flattens for a time, then rises again, but only slightly. When the trail begins to run downhill, look for an unsigned side path on the right (south) at **1.8** miles. Take the right for a brief detour. Shortly it leads to an open, knobby area that is great for a rest and more views. Unfortunately for the viewing, there are lots of wires overhead.

From here, watch your footing carefully, for the trail begins to get out onto the walls of the gorge. If it had not been cut into the rock, there would be no trail at all, and "down" takes on special meaning. It is 800 feet to the bottom

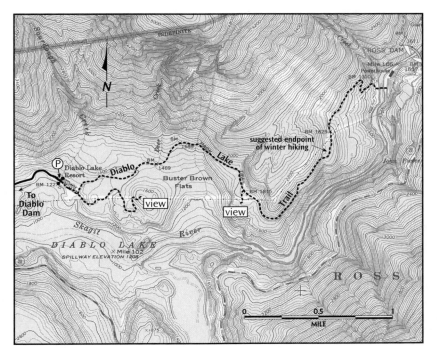

of the gorge and the only remaining stretch of free-running Skagit River in the Cascade Mountains.

The high point (2,000 feet) is of this same collage of great trail, open forest, high mountains, and respect-generating drop-offs. In a bit more than another mile from here, the trail drops gradually to a wide suspension bridge over the river at the Ross Powerhouse. But be aware that during the snowy season you might be stopped on that stretch by the aftermath of massive avalanches. The sound of fearsome water drilling through the snow beneath will be enough to stimulate an overwhelming desire to do that portion of trail another day.

That 2,000-foot-high point, **2.7** miles from the trailhead, is also the high point of the viewing day, and the prudent winter hiking turnaround point as well.

12 Cattle Point

Distance:	3.0 to 5.0 miles total
Time:	3 to 5 hours
Starting elevation:	120 feet
High point:	295 feet
Trail type:	Various: beach walking and trails in open grasslands
Avalanche potential:	None
Difficulty level:	Easy
Maps:	For a road map of the island, call or write San Juan Island National Historic Park, 360-378-2240, P.O. Box 429, Friday Harbor, WA 98250

The Hike

How about some cactus and a natural prairie for a change of pace? No, this outing is not in west Texas or even in eastern Washington, but on San Juan

The Cattle Point Light, on San Juan Island.

Island. You might even spot a golden eagle at Cattle Point, the extreme southeastern tip of the island.

A person could easily spend a whole weekend at Cattle Point, so do it justice in only one day by combining the various walks with driving from stop to stop. The walking distances and times exhibit a wide spread because there are many additional interesting places to explore. With one exception—the lighthouse headland—all of the recommended features are within San Juan Island National Historical Park.

In the 1850s, both the United States and Great Britain's Hudson's Bay Company occupied San Juan Island. It was a peaceful coexistence until an American settler took exception to repeated raids on his veggie patch by one of the Hudson's Bay Company's porkers. He dispatched the troublesome pig, and a royal row ensued. Both nations sent troops.

Fortunately, the Pig War was a boaring affair, for the shot that killed the black tusker was the only one fired. American Camp at Cattle Point and English Camp, later established 15 miles north on Garrison Bay, are now preserved as a national historic park.

Getting There

If you don't have your own boat, water routes to San Juan Island are by the passengers-only *Victoria Clipper* from Seattle, the passengers-only San Juan Island *Shuttle Express* from Bellingham, or the more frequently used Washington State Ferry from Anacortes. You can drive onto the Washington State Ferry or, for even more adventure, leave your car on the mainland and bring a bicycle.

To catch the ferry from Anacortes, drive State Route 20 west from Interstate 5 Exit 230 in Burlington. Where it turns south for Whidbey Island and Deception Pass, continue west on Spur 20 to Anacortes, and follow the signs 4 miles west of town to the ferry terminal. Be sure to catch an early boat in order to make the short daylight hours count.

All the scheduled watercraft mentioned dock at Friday Harbor. Bikes and motor scooters can be rented at the waterfront.

From the ferry landing, go uphill on Spring Street. In 0.5 mile, turn left (south) on Mullis Road, which becomes Argyle Road, then jogs west around the golf course, changing names again to Cattle Point Road. Except for the stretch passing through San Juan Island National Historical Park, renamed American Camp Road, it remains Cattle Point Road to its end. At 5.7 miles from the waterfront is the park boundary and a right turn into the visitors center. Park at the center and explore it first.

The Trail

Exhibits in the visitors center explain in detail the fascinating Pig War story. They set the tone well for what comes next. Directly at the east edge of the parking lot is a pathway through the parade ground and to more historic buildings. Follow it directly east to the Redoubt, the highest hill ahead, for an 0.8-mile round-trip to and from one of the key pieces in the almost-fought war.

The way to the Redoubt travels through some natural prairie. If you go off trail, watch out for rabbit holes as there are zillions on the island (holes *and* rabbits). Not surprisingly, there is a healthy population of red foxes as well. It is not unusual to see one of these sleek predators trotting through the waving grasses. As for cactus, the San Juan brittle cactus is scattered throughout the island. Look for it in drier, well-drained locales.

The Redoubt was a high-ground fortification. General George Pickett, sent out from Bellingham, had his twenty-seven men dig in atop the hill to await an attack that never came. We can't speak for the military angle, but they had the view part right, looking downsound toward Seattle and across the Strait of Juan de Fuca to the Olympic Mountains. The flavor of the wind is that of the open ocean to the west.

Next stop is South Beach. Walk back to your conveyance and drive, pedal, or scoot back out to Cattle Point Road, now American Camp Road. Turn right (east) and go 1.5 miles to Pickett Lane. Turn right (south) on Pickett for the half mile or so to road's end and find plenty of parking at the beach. Mounds of drift logs testify to the power of the winds along this coast. The distance includes a mile for walking west along the beach and back. If time pinches, a dirt road goes the same way.

Before the bends set in with all of this sea-level stuff, it is well to counter the low altitude with some real elevation gain. Mount Finlayson beckons. It is an awesome 295 vertical feet above the beach, and its bulk dominates the eastern horizon (at 82 degrees) from South Beach.

Drive back out to American Camp Road and turn right (east). At 0.5 mile from Pickett Lane park on the shoulder where American Camp Road swings in close to the base of the mountain. There are no signs. Walk up a well-used, grassy service road for an 0.8-mile round-trip to and from the excellent views from Finlayson's top. Most striking are the 32 miles of open water across the strait to Port Angeles. Mount Rainier is always there, if not always visible. Even the top half of Mount Erie is in view, nearly due east, as it thrusts above the low hills of Lopez Island.

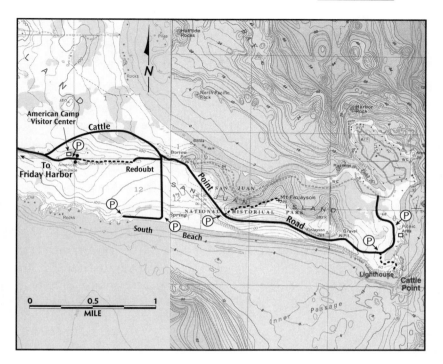

After the high of Mount Finlayson, drive approximately 1.2 miles farther east on American Camp Road for the start of the trail to Cattle Point Lighthouse. The trailhead is signed, but only a very small turnout on the right side of the road provides parking. The lighthouse is visible the entire distance on the driving approach, so its trailhead is not hard to find. The walk is a half mile round-trip, and the route is nicely signed with ecological information.

From the light, look east to Iceberg Point at the southern tip of Lopez Island, and gaze west to the outlines of British Columbia's Vancouver Island. The Pacific Ocean is not far beyond there.

One more stop lies a few hundred yards east of the lighthouse trailhead. Walk or ride to this day-use interpretive area on San Juan Channel. During the 1920s, the building, now a picnic shelter, housed a wireless radio station to aid ships coming and going through the Strait of Juan de Fuca. The entrance to Puget Sound is Admiralty Inlet, southeast of the wireless station, and navigators in fogbound waters needed to know exactly where to make the turn. There was likely some amount of panic in those requests for bearings from Cattle Point.

13 West-side Adventures

Distance:	3.0 miles total
Time:	5 hours
Starting elevation:	50 feet
High point:	650 feet
Trail type:	Various: forest trails, park walks, open ledges
Avalanche potential:	None
Difficulty level:	Easy to moderate
Map:	USGS Roche Harbor (7.5' series), or call San Juan Island National Historical Park, 360-378-2240, to request a road map of the island (P.O. Box 429, Friday Harbor, WA 98250)

The light at Lime Kiln Point, on the west shore of San Juan Island.

The Hike

The west shore of San Juan Island is more rugged and less settled than many other parts of the island. The number of places to visit along the road make this outing more of a driving tour with walking stops than a single hike. The information above summarizes the walking portions of three destinations.

This west-side adventure begins with a history walk and a great leg-stretching climb of Young Mountain, both right out of the parking area for English Camp, stop number one.

English Camp became the home turf of the Royal Marines in an almost - war in which the first and only shot killed a pig. The shooter was an American settler defending his vegetable patch, and the shootee was a hapless hog belonging to the Hudson's Bay Company. It happened at the south end of the island, but as the affair cooled the Royal Marines moved 15 miles north to establish English Camp on Garrison Bay.

Getting There

Practically speaking, access to San Juan Island is by water, and all conveyances dock at Friday Harbor, including the passengers-only *Victoria Clipper* from Seattle, the San Juan Island *Shuttle Express* from Bellingham, and the Washington State Ferry, which brings vehicles, walk-ons, and bicyclists from Anacortes. For driving directions to the Anacortes ferry, see Hike 12.

In Friday Harbor, go uphill through town on Spring Street. Two blocks from the waterfront, turn right on Second Street. In three more blocks, cross Blair Avenue onto Guard Street. Soon the way becomes Beaverton Valley Road. With one more name change to West Valley Road, this route goes all the way to English Camp. (Don't be surprised if some signs call it "British" Camp.) At 8.3 miles, turn left into the entrance to the camp in San Juan Island National Historical Park.

The Trail

Tour the park site by walking down to the visitors center and some tended gardens. Walk the grounds amid mostly original buildings, and imagine the sloops and frigates rocking in the sheltered bay. It must have been lonely duty for those so far from home.

Return to the parking area and walk to its east end. There, pick up the trail to all 650 vertical feet of Young Mountain. Tramp upward for **0.2** mile and cross West Valley Road. Shortly after the usual trail info sign, **0.3** mile along, the trail splits. The left fork is summit bound, but the right branch is signed for British Cemetery, only a 0.1-mile diversion. It is humbling to view the graves of people whose souls could not await return to England for release. The most legible stone is that of G. E. Stewart, a corporal in the Royal Marines, "who suddenly departed this life" on June 1, 1865. Most of those buried at the site died in drowning accidents.

The other reason for trekking to the white-fenced plot is to see some of the old and deeply furrowed Garry oaks in the area. Sadly, these somewhat rare monarchs are no longer reproducing well. When gone, no little white fence will be built for them.

Go back to the main trail and turn right and upward on the summit route. Note the increasing numbers of broad-leaved and evergreen madrona trees along the way. These beauties peel naturally to reveal different browns, tans, and greens in their underbark. Though they appear from southern California to southwestern British Columbia, they grow in greater concentrations in coastal Oregon and Washington.

At **0.9** mile, just shy of the summit, a short trail leads right and onto a broad ledge with excellent views west and north. Down below is Garrison Bay, shielded against winds coming off Haro Strait and justifying the site of English Camp.

The trail is increasingly on moss-draped bedrock. Stay off the moss as much as possible, please. Imagine how long it takes to grow such a gorgeous mantle, and imagine how quickly it is scuffed away by errant feet.

More views appear from the top in another tenth of a mile, all to the south and west. At 177 degrees, nearly due south, stands Dallas Mountain, likely the high point on the island at 1,090 feet. Thirty-five miles away, over the churning waters of the Strait of Juan de Fuca, sits Port Angeles with its backdrop of Hurricane Ridge and Olympic National Park. To the west is Vancouver Island, as well as a few of the Gulf Islands, Canada's equivalent of the San Juans.

Off the mountain at the parking area, reset your odometer. The trip back to Friday Harbor consists of a route along the west coast of the island and two more short walks. Leave English Camp and turn right (south) on West Valley Road. Soon go right (west) onto Mitchell Bay Road. At 3.1 miles from the camp, turn left (south) on West Side Road. Take a right turn at 4.9 miles, and drive down into San Juan County Park, a delightful place on a tiny cove with a sand beach to match. By all means, take the **0.8**-mile round-trip walk out onto the headland on the northwest side of the bay. Saunter back to your conveyance when you must, and get ready for the next stop at Lime Kiln Point State Park.

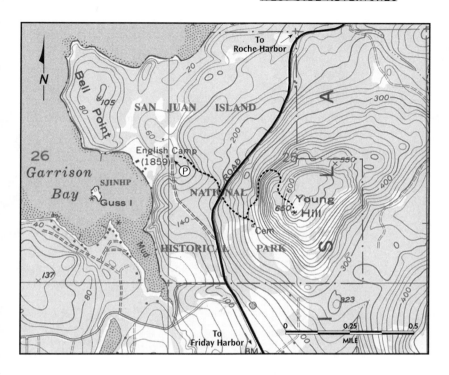

Leaving San Juan County Park, maintain the mileage count and continue south on West Side Road. At 7.6 miles, on the outside of a tight curve at the bottom of a hill, turn right (north) and into the park.

Lime Kiln Point State Park is a bare-bones day-use facility with a picturesque lighthouse. In addition to the **0.6**-mile walk out and back from the lighthouse, the park often features something else big: orcas. The downside is that the whales are mostly seen June through August. Prowl the grounds, enjoy the view (strain your eyes anyway for spouts), and put Lime Kiln on your other-season calendar for a revisit.

Leave the park with the same odometer count, again heading south on West Side Road. For a couple of miles the road hovers over the turbulent meeting of Haro and Juan de Fuca Straits before turning inland. At 10.8 miles, turn left (north) on Wold Road, then right (east) on San Juan Valley Road at the 13.9-mile point. It will run right down Spring Street in Friday Harbor and back to the ferry dock in 4.0 more miles.

14 Shark Reef Sanctuary

Distance:	0.7 mile round-trip
Time:	1 to 2 hours
Starting elevation:	40 feet
High point:	40 feet
Trail type:	Forest walk to rocky coast
Avalanche potential:	None
Difficulty level:	Easy
Map:	USGS Richardson (7.5' series), or order a road map (which will be sufficient) from the Lopez Chamber of Commerce (P.O. Box 102, Lopez Island, WA 98261)

Fences at the end of the cliffside jaunt at Shark Reef Sanctuary.

The Hike

Enjoy the misty isle cruise and the drive along time-lapsed island roads, but heighten your chances of a welcoming attitude from the residents by keeping to the public areas of Lopez Island. At times, the proliferation of "Keep Out," "No Trespassing," and "Respect Our Privacy" signs seems to suggest they would rather the mainlanders stay away, but the unthinking among us have brought it all about. Keep to the public lands, and the warm island ambience will suffuse your stay.

Getting There

To get to Lopez, take the Washington State Ferry from Anacortes. (For driving directions to the ferry terminal, see Hike 12.)

On Lopez, the one road leading away from the ferry dock is named, not surprisingly, Ferry Road. Drive to its end in 2.0 miles, passing Odlin County Park along the way. Turn right onto Fisherman Bay Road to the 8.0-mile mark to another T. While traveling along Fisherman Bay Road, consider a short detour through Lopez Village. It has lots of gift and supply shops and a good grocery store. The Bay Cafe is a pleasing lunch stop. Reception in the village is very friendly.

Go right on Davis Bay Road. At 9.2 miles, turn right a third time, onto Burt Road. Getting close! In just 2.0 more miles, intersect Shark Reef Road and go left into the park. Find the trailhead parking and rest rooms on the right at 10.4 miles. The road continues, but only to private property.

The Trail

It is only a quarter mile to the water, but anticipation mounts as you approach. Crashing waves tell all. Do not hurry through the trees, though, because the coastal forest of Douglas fir and lodgepole pine is quite different from what most of us are used to. It has an "island" feel to it.

West across the rough channel is Cattle Point on San Juan Island. Beyond that landfall, looking south across the Strait of Juan de Fuca, lies Port Angeles with its Olympic Mountains backdrop. The waters off land's end seem always to be angry at this juncture, as if the currents in the strait running to and from the Pacific are resentful of those that squeeze from between the islands, confusing an orderly flow. That open ocean is not so far away.

Stroll the windswept bench to the southeast until halted by barbed wire. There is no beach, but Shark Reef doesn't need one. Its charm is in continuous

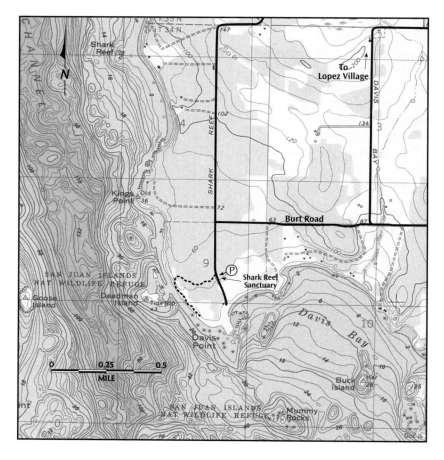

bedrock ledges 15 feet above the waves. Offshore is a rock mass called Deadman Island. Such imagery—sharks, reefs, and now "Deadman Island"! The latter is one of many islands in the archipelago of the San Juan Islands National Wildlife Refuge. All are havens for birds, seals, and sea lions. As for sharks, you are about as likely to glimpse one as you are to see a Jolly Roger hove into view around the tip of Deadman Island.

Watch that ferry schedule. Sailings are infrequent from Lopez.

15 Mount Constitution

Distance:	5.2 miles round-trip
Time:	3 hours
Starting elevation:	2,000 feet
High point:	2,409 feet
Trail type:	Through forest and along cliff tops to summit
Avalanche potential:	None
Difficulty level:	Easy to moderate
Maps:	Moran State Park Map and Trail Guide or USGS Mount Constitution (7.5' series)

The Hike

Even at the modest height of 2,409 feet, Mount Constitution is a big and rugged mountain. The peak's massive underlayment of bedrock is starkly evident, often protruding through a thin veneer of soil. The result? An already incomparable island mystique is brushstroked to perfection by vistas from parapetlike cliff tops and a solid rock summit.

Getting There

To reach Orcas Island, take the Washington State Ferry from Anacortes. (For driving directions to the ferry terminal, see Hike 12.) When you arrive on Orcas, drive 9.0 miles to the town of East Sound, then proceed 1.0 mile east to a stop sign. A right turn (south) leads to the north entrance of Moran State Park in a total of 13.5 miles from the ferry. Keep going. At 14.8 miles take the left fork at a Y, now on Summit Road.

At 17.8 miles park in a graveled turnout on the right, signed "Little Summit Trail Head." If you reach Cold Springs Trail, you have gone a mile too far.

The Trail

Barely into the woods, trending eastward, a side trail goes right, leading to Little Summit. It is a gorgeous diversion that casts the eye more to the west than is true for the big summit; up top, views are mostly from northeast to

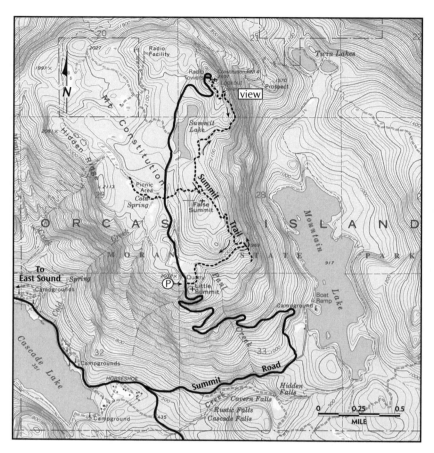

southwest. Besides, the 0.2-mile round-trip diversion is already figured into the mileage.

Back on the main trail, in **0.4** mile total an old road sweeps in from the left. It isn't signed, so turn and look at it, to be sure you make the correct choice on the way back.

You reach a trail junction at **0.6** mile. The elevation here is 1,940 feet, slightly lower than the parking area. Go left. From the junction it is 2.0 miles to the summit, but long before that the way courses along the tops of south-facing cliffs where the views are sizzling.

After rounding to the east side of the peak, still on cliff-top extravaganza, the trail switchbacks a couple of times before reaching the cluster of summit buildings and the very photogenic stone viewing tower.

As for the views? Superlatives utterly fail. It's a fairy-tale vision of bejeweled islands cast upon the sparkling waters of Puget Sound. Much of Whatcom County's shoreline and mountains, too, spread out to the east. Feed opportunistic ravens, and look down on soaring eagles. East beneath Mount Constitution's cliffs sit Twin Lakes, with the larger Mountain Lake off to the southeast, and all in the large state park.

You cannot help taking home an eyeful, but whether on film or in the mind, the images will never measure up to being there.

16 | Fidalgo Head Loop Trail

Distance:	2.4 miles round-trip
Time:	2 to 3 hours
Starting elevation:	0 feet
High point:	220 feet
Trail type:	Shoreline and forest trail to rocky bluffs
Avalanche potential:	None
Difficulty level:	Easy to moderate
Map:	USGS Deception Pass (7.5' series), though none is needed

The Hike

Fidalgo Head is the westernmost extension of Fidalgo Island, and the home turf of the city of parks, Anacortes. The entire headland is preserved as delightful Washington Park, and it has something for nearly everyone seeking

Burrows Pass and Island, from Fidalgo Head Loop Trail.

outdoor pursuits. There are beaches, a boat launch, a picnic area, a campground, a scenic drive, and, best of all, a loop trail with side jaunts to the water's edge and a rocky overlook.

The vexing part of doing the Fidalgo Head Loop Trail is in finding the trailhead once in the park. One end of the trail is totally unsigned, and while the other end is marked, nowhere on any of the park's directional signs is the trail's existence acknowledged.

Getting There

Drive State Route 20 west for 12 miles from Interstate 5 Exit 230. Leave SR 20 and continue straight ahead on Spur 20 to downtown Anacortes. Follow the San Juan Island ferry signs 4.0 miles west of downtown, then go another mile and drive right into Washington Park.

Three short roadways, all right turns where you can find parking, start at the park entrance. The first is a picnic area, the second is marked "Beach," and the third is a boat launch with paid parking. All three share the same small beach.

Opposite the second, or beach-area parking entry, is the unsigned end of the trail. Skip this and start at the beginning of the loop, farther down the beach. That way you'll save the best for later in the ascent and also proceed in sequence with the trail-sign mileages.

The Trail

Walk to the extreme west end of the beach. The trail starts where sand and grass end and forest begins, literally at sea level. The park road, just above, also makes a loop around the headland, but it goes to some different places. It is highly recommended that you also make the drive.

The north side of the park faces Guemes Channel, and the land mass most directly across the water is Cypress Island. In **0.2** mile the trail leaves the shore and crosses the loop road. A signed side trail at the crossing indicates the way to Green Point, but Green and another destination, West Beach, coming up soon, are best left for the driving tour. You won't be cheated of views since up on the headland the trail goes to some viewpoints the road does not.

Across the road the route continues on flat ground in mature forest. Douglas fir predominates, but western red cedar is much in evidence as well. Salal makes a luxurious groundcover.

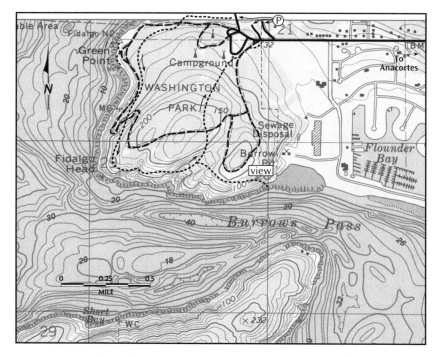

At **0.6** mile the trail starts climbing noticeably and crosses the loop road. Another tenth of a mile brings you to a junction with the Juniper Point Trail. (The 0.2-mile round-trip to the point and back is included in the 2.4 miles calculated for total distance.) Out on the point, look across Burrows Pass to the end of its namesake island. To the right of Burrows Island is wide Rosario Strait.

Back on the main trail the mile count, including the side trip, is **0.9**. At **1.3** miles is the junction with the Burrows Trail, a 0.6-mile side trip (also in the total distance) and a nice change of pace. It really is on the channel—and worth it in spite of losing 220 vertical feet.

Back up at the junction (**1.9** miles total) cross the driving loop road again at the **2.0**-mile mark and start the downhill glide. Come to the road a final time at **2.3** miles, this time with no hint of which way to go. There is more of the trail, but it is confusing. It is best to walk down the road, for your vehicle will be right around the corner.

17 SKAGIT COUNTY
Mount Erie

🥾🥾🥾🥾🥾

Distance: 4.8 miles round-trip
Time: 5 hours
Starting elevation: 390 feet
High point: 1,270 feet
Trail type: Through forest to summit views
Avalanche potential: None
Difficulty level: Moderate to strenuous
Map: USGS Deception Pass (7.5' series)

The Hike

Mount Erie is a veritable jewel. The mountain has such distinctive relief from all of its surrounding terrain that it is a landmark from numerous points in four northern counties. Its summit is wooded, but four viewing platforms have been constructed, corresponding roughly to the cardinal directions. The result is stunning vistas in all directions.

Getting There

Take Interstate 5 Exit 230 in Burlington, State Route 20, and drive west. When SR 20 turns left (south) to Whidbey Island in 12 miles, continue straight on Spur 20. Where the freeway ends, the traffic swings north to head for downtown Anacortes, but in just 0.3 mile (14.7 miles from I-5), turn left (west) on 34th Street. At 15.2 miles, turn left (south) on H Avenue for another half mile. H Avenue ends there at 41st Street but continues as Heart Lake Road. Keep going south on Heart Lake Road.

At 17.7 miles from I-5, turn left onto a paved turnout loop road. Sugarloaf Trail 215 and the beginning of the summit auto road are side by side at the midpoint of the loop. You will find lots of parking.

The Trail

Trails in the Anacortes Community Forest Lands (ACFL) are like peanut shells outside a monkey cage: They are everywhere. For this hike you really need to bring this trail description with you or, better yet, get a copy of the trail-system map from ACFL. (See Resources, at end of the book.)

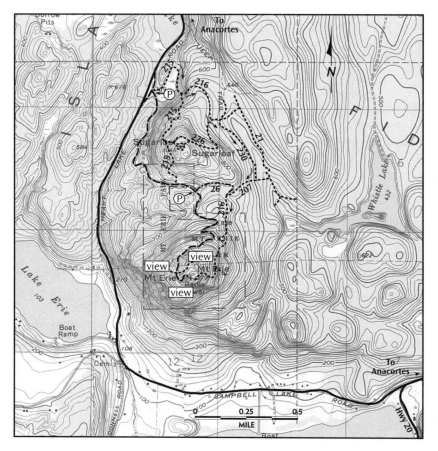

The start of Sugarloaf Trail 215 is deceptively flat, but it soon climbs. In **0.4** mile leave Trail 215 and go left at a Y on Trail 225. (Trail 215 goes to the summit of Sugarloaf.)

At **0.8** mile Trail 225 comes to a T junction with Trail 226 coming down off Sugarloaf. Go left (northeast) on Trail 226, but only for 0.1 mile.

At **0.9** mile is a second T. Go right (southeast) on Trail 230, which begins to descend in deep, dark woods as you get close to the base of Mount Erie. At **1.4** miles, take the right fork at an unsigned junction onto a crossover trail that avoids the very boggy old junction downhill. In less than a tenth of a mile the crossover intersects Trail 207. Go right (west) and start climbing in earnest, at last on the mountain.

At **1.7** miles, Trail 26 enters from the right. It is very wide, and apparently an old forest road. Go left (southwest). Though unsigned, this is Trail 226. The mountainside is increasingly knobby and rough, but the trail is easy to follow. Don't have a coronary if a straining car roars past off to the right. The summit road is very close.

At **1.9** miles (1,120 feet) the trail has finished climbing steeply for a time as an unsigned path enters from the left just before massive blowdown. Though optional, take the left trail for a quarter-mile round-trip and a real treat. For some unknown reason, a 30-inch-thick Douglas fir has grown a 20-inch-thick limb relatively close to the ground. Reach forward, not upward, to touch. The errant appendage doesn't turn upward for light until it is some 35 feet from mom.

Go back to the main trail at Big Limb Junction and head left for the summit through the hacked-away blowdown. As in many popular parks, unofficial trails and shortcuts become legion. Signage takes a beating, too. Just keep track of how you did it, and, of course, take pride in knowing . . . you did it your way. The top is **2.4** miles total from the trailhead, including the jaunt to Big Limb.

The south observation point looks out over Campbell Lake toward Deception Pass and down Whidbey Island. For views westward into the San Juans, stroll the paths along cliff tops above rock climbers, or watch the parasailers take their leaps of faith into space. More eaglelike vistas abound from the west observation point. For breathtaking sights north and east, walk a short way down the auto road to small turnouts left and right. Walkways lead to observation points. All constructed view sites have good identification photos.

18 | Whistle Lake

Distance:	3.5 miles round-trip
Time:	3 hours
Starting elevation:	340 feet
High point:	740 feet
Trail type:	Forest trails around a lake
Avalanche potential:	None
Difficulty level:	Easy to moderate
Map:	Anacortes Community Forest Lands Trail Guide (see Resources) or USGS Anacortes South (7.5' series)

The Hike

Whistle Lake, part of the Anacortes Community Forest Lands (ACFL), is really two different kinds of water bodies joined together. The north end is a typical woodland lake, but the south portion, the outlet end, is a microcanyonland of deep and quiet coves and passageways.

Getting There

Drive State Route 20 west from Interstate 5 Exit 230 in Burlington. Where SR 20 turns south to Oak Harbor, continue west on Spur 20 toward Anacortes. At the end of Spur 20 (14.4 miles from I-5), turn left at Commercial Street (not right as if for downtown).

Reset your odometer. Turns come quickly. Go one block on Commercial and turn left (east) on 37th Street for three more blocks. Turn right (south) uphill on S Street for one block (about 0.4 mile so far). Turn left (east) on 38th Street, which narrows to a lanelike street for four blocks, then curves south as V Avenue with nice views over March Point to the east. After two blocks on V, jog left for a wink, then, at 0.7 mile, turn south on Whistle Lake Road.

At 1.7 total miles Whistle Lake Road ends. Turn left on Whistle Lake Terrace for only 0.1 mile. At 1.8 miles, leave Whistle Lake Terrace for a gravel road to the right. Take the right fork of a Y in about 0.1 mile. At 2.1 miles from that first left onto Commercial Street, enter the parking area for three ACFL trailheads.

The Trail

The leftmost of three trail choices is the Jerry Wallrath Trail, actually a service and fire road to the head of the lake. On the ACFL map it is also shown as Trail 20. Whistle Lake used to be the water supply for Anacortes, and portions of the old iron pipe are visible here and there in the roadbed. In **0.7** mile, ignoring several side trails, the road reaches the north end of the lake. Stay left on Trail 20, which continues down the east shore.

Trail 20 ends on a small sandy point along the lake. Find Trail 205 at the rear of the clearing and continue. Trail 205 comprises about half of the lake circuit and most of the rough part of the trail. After rounding a small cove at the southeast corner of the main body of Whistle Lake, the route turns west. In succession it passes through old, cut-away blowdown, accepts the entry of Trail 217 from the left (east), and starts gaining elevation. You are still on Trail 205 and headed west. The junction with Trail 217 represents the **1.2**-mile mark of the circumnavigation of Whistle Lake.

The route becomes more interesting, for the track is now on knobby, ice-carved bedrock ledges, so common and so charming in the island country. It is also this character that forms the ruggedness of the outlet end of the lake.

Atop the knobs (high point 740 feet), boot-driven paths lead off in the direction of the lake but cope poorly with the brush and the ledges. A better opportunity lies ahead. Down about a hundred vertical feet from the high point, a well-used side trail goes off to the right. From a bluff some 50 feet above the water, good views extend both ways along the outlet channel. Return to Trail 205. Stay right at one unsigned trail junction, and go down to cross the outlet stream. You are not quite halfway around the lake, and the best is yet to come.

The outlet runs directly into Toot Swamp, and the trail (now Trail 23) follows all of the swamp's north shore on its way to a junction with Trail 206 at the **1.6**-mile mark of the hike. Signs here do not say so, but old friend Two Oh Five is still with you. Anyway, go right and to another junction less than a quarter mile away, this time to turn right again on Trail 22. This is the **1.8**-mile point.

Lots of short stretches with lots of different numbers characterize this stretch of trail. Their purpose is to get us headed back northward on the most scenic route.

Go for only a quarter mile on Trail 22, and turn right again on Trail 21. In 0.1 mile Trail 202 crosses the path. Take it to the right and downhill all the

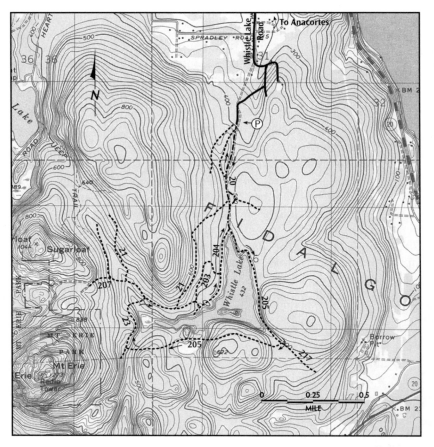

way to the lake, and the **2.1**-mile mark. (At about 100 feet above the water, you get a great introduction to the labyrinthine ways of the outlet canyon.)

Go back up Trail 202 a short distance to Trail 204, which you likely saw on the way down. Take Trail 204 to the right (north). The trail undulates along the west shore of the lake with lots more stolen glimpses into mysterious bays and passages. Along the way, Trail 203 comes in from the left, and at one point Trail 204 nearly touches Trail 21, but stay with the views. Doubtless, that last part goes without saying.

Back at the north end of the lake the **2.8**-mile circle is complete, and it is an easy 0.7 mile along the Jerry Wallrath Trail to the car.

The Trails of Blanchard Mountain

Explore early logging railway history, watch eagles soar with hang gliders, and delve into a geological puzzle on a high cliff. Blanchard is a big mountain, and there are many days of varied hiking experiences to be enjoyed on its flanks.

Big as it is, though, you might not find it—on the map, that is. USGS shows it on both the Bow and the Bellingham South topos as Chuckanut Mountain— erroneously, we think.

As for the Chuckanut designation, any peaklet would be proud to bear the name, but there is a 1,700-foot drop from the summit of Blanchard to the valley of Oyster Creek that separates the two landforms.

Hikers owe some thank-yous to the Back Country Horsemen's Association for good volunteer bridge and trail work on the Blanchard Hill Trail (Hike 22). (We won't argue the hill versus mountain part; it's on all the signs as "Hill.") More applause, please, for the Pacific Northwest Trail Association. Its members have done the same good work plus put up great signage in many places.

This book features four trails on this mountainous hill named Blanchard. The first is the Oyster Dome, Hike 19, via the Pacific Northwest Trail on Chuckanut Drive. The next three hikes share the same access road, and two of those start out at the same trailhead.

19 The Oyster Dome

Distance:	8.0 miles round-trip
Time:	5.5 hours
Starting elevation:	160 feet
High point:	2,000 feet
Trail type:	Climbs steeply, upper portion rough
Avalanche potential:	None
Difficulty level:	Moderate to strenuous
Map:	USGS Bellingham South and USGS Bow (7.5' series)

The Hike

The *Oyster* Dome? What kind of a place could *that* be? To say that it is a 300-foot cliff with views out over a good chunk of Northwest creation is the public relations answer. And right on as well. The plain truth is, though, nobody knows how the landform came into being.

Getting There

From the south, in Burlington, take Interstate 5 Exit 231, signed Chuckanut Drive and State Route 11, and drive north to milepost 10. Park on the paved left shoulder. From Bellingham, take I-5 Exit 252, the north end of SR 11. Drive west about a mile to a traffic light at 12th Street where SR 11 turns left (south). Approximately 12.0 miles from I-5, and within sight of MP 10, park on the paved right shoulder.

The Trail

The Pacific Northwest Trail (PNT) starts across the road from the long, narrow parking turnout and is plainly marked with white vertical bars painted on trees and rocks. Double bars designate abrupt changes of direction, such as switchbacks and trail junctions. PNT volunteers have done a superb job of making the newer first half of the trail rarely more than moderately steep.

At about **1.0** mile, the trail breaks out of deep woods into a large clear-cut. Views are a hint of what is to come. Look upward, too, for bald eagles are

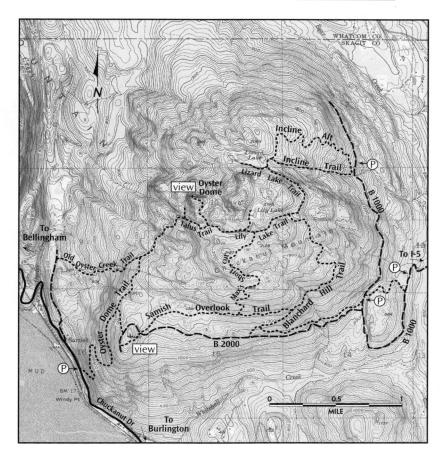

common along the intertidal zone in winter. The really big flyers are more likely hang gliders; Samish Overlook and launch site is right upslope.

At **1.9** miles the trail reaches a junction. The Connector Trail leads right (south) to Samish Overlook, but for now stay straight ahead on the way to the dome.

In another half mile the PNT ends at the Old Oyster Creek Trail coming up from below. (The old trail's beginning is lost in a welter of new homes.) The junction is **2.5** miles from the trailhead and at 1,280 feet. Turn right on Old Oyster Creek Trail and begin the ascent in earnest. More of everything: rougher, steeper, muddier.

At **3.2** miles, the very steep trail reaches a side path left (north), signed for Talus Trail, to the Bat Caves. Pass it by for now. You will likely insist on going in on the way down, after hearing more about the Oyster Dome.

It is only a quarter mile more to a junction with the Rock Trail, **3.5** miles from Chuckanut Drive. Follow it left (north) to the Oyster Dome in another half mile, **4.0** miles in all and 2,000 feet above the bay.

The Dome is a sheer wall of rock some 300 feet high. Its top is a sloping shelf about 150 feet long. Of course, the upper end, as high as one can go, is the only place to be.

The entire San Juans archipelago and more unfold before your disbelieving eyes. Sweep the expanse of the Skagit River Delta to the south, then out over Samish Bay below.

You are staring at large chunks of four counties. On a clear day, the white-capped Olympics provide a backdrop to the entire south half of the view west. And who knows how many slices of Canada's Gulf Islands are out there beyond the San Juans?

The Oyster Dome is a geological mystery. Whatever happened was cataclysmic for sure. Down below you rests a jumble of gigantic stone blocks. The pile suggests that the cliff was once a big knob whose west half simply exploded and collapsed. The area at the foot of the cliff, a tenth of a mile out the Talus Trail, is known as the Bat Caves. Though it does house lots of bats in its convoluted passageways, there are no true caves. Its other delights are summed up by a sign that greets the hiker on arrival at the first mammoth boulders: "Enter at your own risk. Dangers include cold water–induced fatigue and hypothermia, animal or human feces, broken glass, corrosives, drowning, a multilevel maze of small, muddy crawls amid loose rocks and pits, rockfall, speleophobia, skunk dens, and toxic calcium carbide."

The sign is not a warning to stay out of the Bat Caves area, only out of its dangerous maze of below-ground passageways. Do hike in the short way to see the wow-some jumble of huge stone blocks, but resist becoming the object of another Bat Caves rescue attempt. There have been a few of them.

20 Samish Overlook

Distance:	5.5 miles round-trip
Time:	3.75 hours
Starting elevation:	820 feet
High point:	1,460 feet
Trail type:	Gentle to occasionally moderate up and down, lots of contouring
Avalanche potential:	None
Difficulty level:	Easy to moderate
Maps:	USGS Bow and USGS Alger (7.5' series)

The Hike

Samish Overlook, a 1,300-foot bulge at the southwest end of Blanchard Mountain, is a virtual hang-glider base with three or four launching pads. In between takeoffs and eagle flyovers, spectators get to look down upon the monopoly board of farms and out over the world of island living beyond.

Hang glider launching pad at Samish Overlook.

The eagles appear to consider the gliders as kin and frequently can be seen matching them circle for circle as soaring equals.

See page 61 for the map showing this hike.

Getting There

Drive Interstate 5 to Alger Exit 240. Reset your odometer and go left over the overpass (northwest) on Samish Lake Road for 0.4 mile to Barrel Springs Road. Turn left and drive to a right turn (west) onto a gravel forest road at 1.1 miles from I-5. The road is signed for Road B-1000 and also Blanchard Hill Trails. Drive upward to a large graveled parking area at 1.6 miles, but don't dismount yet.

Though you may park here for the lower trailhead, and while it's okay to start here (the walking start is 500 feet farther along the road), this access is primarily used by horse riders. It is 1.0 mile by trail from here, or 1.6 miles by vehicle, to the upper trailhead.

If you drive on, ignore a side road (B-2000) left (west) just before spotting the upper trailhead, also on the left, at 2.7 miles from I-5. Ample parking is found 0.1 mile uphill from the start of the trail.

The Trail

From parking, walk **0.1** mile downhill to the start of the Blanchard Hill Trail. Trail signs at the start do not mention the overlook, but a route change along Blanchard Hill Trail will put things right. The trail parallels Road B-2000 but is always above it. It climbs slowly on the edge of mature forest to **0.7** mile, then begins to steepen and pull away from the road. The climb remains moderate to 1,420 feet in elevation, at **1.5** miles, to a junction with the Samish Overlook Trail. An old sign also mentions the PNT, or Pacific Northwest Trail, and might one day be renamed the Larry Reed Trail. Go left (west). After topping out at 1,460 feet in about 0.2 mile, the overlook route stays close to the 1,400-foot mark for more than a mile.

At **2.3** miles is another junction, this time with Max's Shortcut, coming from the north and down from Lily Lake. Continue straight on. Max's is part of the present-day Pacific Northwest Trail Association's plan to link Montana with the Washington coast, so from the junction on, the trail to the overlook will have single, white, rectangular PNT blazes.

The route begins to drop gradually to a saddle at **2.6** miles, then even more until it comes out of the trees in a 1980s clear-cut at 1,280 feet in elevation. In another 0.1 mile, **2.9** miles into the walk, the trail crosses Road B-2000 and enters another stand of mature trees. Samish Overlook, the **3.2**-mile point of the trip, is only a quarter mile away.

The overlook is a linear affair spread along a quarter mile of Road B-2000. The trail comes out of the woods at its extreme southern end and close to a turnaround literally on the brink. Start your view tour here, for the panoramas wrap around to the southeast only from this particular launch site.

Due south is Chuckanut Drive, tapering out to Interstate 5 at Burlington. Right below are the tracks of the Burlington Northern Railway. Good old Mount Erie, with its faithful and lower-profile companion Sugarloaf, is in place to the southeast (222 degrees). Move on, for there is much more.

Walk the road upward (north) or cut across lots, but either way view opportunities multiply. Sights out over the San Juans, as well as many islands of Island County, are magnificent. The closest of the non-Juans is Samish Island. Aiming at its middle, which looks skinny enough to break in two at any moment, the bearing is southwest (250 degrees). Continue up the road. Higher is even more spectacular. Look north and see the coastline of steep-sided Chuckanut Mountain with its scenic drive and railroad threading along together. Mount Constitution on Orcas Island is to the northwest (285 degrees).

The last launch and view site is near the top of the hill and a quarter mile from where the trail came out of the woods. From the crest of the hill, look northeast and easily spot the Oyster Dome (Hike 19) off to the left of the road.

It's tough to turn your back on such beauty, but head east and down to where the road intersects the trail, **3.6** miles into the trip.

It's decision time. Back on trail in 2.9 miles? Or go with the road, a mile shorter with more great views, this time new ones to the south? If you stay with the road, dip downward steeply and then rise again, all in the forest. In a scant quarter mile the scenario changes, for the view management teams (loggers) have been at it again, and the world opens out to prairies and sound on one hand and little hills grading to 3,000- and 4,000-footers on the other. From one grassy turnout, **4.2** total miles (1,240 feet elevation), spot Cultus Mountain. It is another winter hike (Hike 27), even though just 7 feet shy of 4,000 feet, and is to the southeast on a bearing of 136 degrees.

From there, clump happily down (and up) Road B-2000 to its junction with the main access road. Turn left (north) on Road B-1000, pass the trailhead in 0.1 mile, and arrive at the sag wagon in another tenth, **5.5** miles for the day.

21 Incline Trail

Distance:	6.4 miles round-trip
Time:	3.5 hours
Starting elevation:	1,050 feet
High point:	2,140 feet
Trail type:	Walk to two mountain lakes in forest
Avalanche potential:	None
Difficulty level:	One-third moderate, two-thirds easy
Map:	USGS Bellingham South and USGS Bow (7.5' series)

The Hike

Mountain lakes have always had a great pull on hikers, and Lizard and Lily Lakes, high on Blanchard Mountain, are no exceptions. Both can be enjoyed at length in a relatively easy day trip.

The Incline Trail is the site of a straight-up-the-fall-line cable car pull in the early logging years of Blanchard Mountain.

See page 61 for the map showing this hike.

Getting There

To reach the trailhead, follow the driving directions given for Samish Overlook, Hike 20. When you reach the road signed for Road B-1000 and also Blanchard Hill Trails, drive upward, past a large graveled parking area at 1.6 miles. Ignore a side road (B-2000) left (west) just before spotting the upper trailhead, also on the left, at 2.7 miles from I-5. From there, continue driving north on Road B-1000. In 1.2 more miles (gaining another 250 feet in precious elevation) find the Incline Trail on the left (west) side of the road. There is parking on the right slightly beyond the trailhead.

The Trail

Immediately inside the woods the trail splits. Although the left fork follows the old cable car route 0.8 mile upward to join an old road, the route is quite eroded and downright unpleasant, for it was never intended to be a walking trail. The right fork, the Incline Alternate, is only 0.4 mile longer and is far more enjoyable. It takes you to the same old road, likely a railroad bed, where you turn left (south) just as if you had come up the Incline directly. Most of the way to both lakes is virtually flat from this point. Once on the old road, pass the upper terminus of the Incline Trail.

At the **1.3**-mile mark the path reaches a junction with the Lizard Lake Trail on the right. It is 0.4 mile in to this secluded little lake at the **1.7**-mile point. Apparently the fishing is good, too, for often two or three folks will be dipping flies.

Back on the main trail, with a total of **2.1** miles behind you, continue south (right) on the same route, now called the Lily and Lizard Lakes Trail. At **2.7** miles is an important trail junction where the Blanchard Hill Trail comes up from the south and tees into your route. From the junction, it is only another half mile straight ahead to Lily Lake.

Lily Lake is the **3.2**-mile mark of the hike, but the nicest surprise is still ahead. Where the outlet stream crosses beneath the trail at the lake's western end is a spur trail leading to the north. It's only 0.4 mile round-trip but leads to another small lake, this one with the feeling that somehow it is all your own.

22 Blanchard Hill Trail

Distance:	7.6 miles round-trip
Time:	6 hours
Starting elevation:	850 feet
High point:	2,140 feet
Trail type:	Rises gently to moderately through forest
Avalanche potential:	None
Difficulty level:	Moderate
Map:	USGS Bellingham South and USGS Bow (7.5' series)

The Hike

Blanchard Hill Trail leads to a popular mountain lake named Lily. This fine trail is on state Department of Natural Resources land but is maintained jointly by that agency and a lot of volunteer help.

See page 61 for the map showing this hike.

Getting There

Follow the driving directions given for Samish Overlook, Hike 20. Use the same upper trailhead described for Samish Overlook.

The Trail

The footpath leads west from Road B-1000, closely paralleling Road B-2000 for about **0.7** mile. It then drifts slowly away, and climbs more moderately. After one major switchback, it comes to a junction with the Samish Overlook Trail at the **1.5**-mile mark. This route, a left (west), may be signed as the Larry Reed Trail. Stay straight ahead (northeast) with the Blanchard Hill Trail.

At the **3.1**-mile point, Blanchard Hill Trail ends at a T junction with the Lily and Lizard Lakes Trail. Turn left (west), now on virtually flat terrain, reaching Lily Lake, and its outlet at the lake's western end, in another half mile.

For an even nicer bit of solitude, take the side trail from where the outlet stream passes beneath the Lily Lake Trail and follow it north for the final 0.2 mile (**3.6** miles from the car) to another small water world. Plunk down on your own quiet piece of backwater shoreline, and enjoy this charming lake.

23
The Alger Alp

Distance: 3.7 miles round-trip
Time: 3 hours
Starting elevation: 300 feet
High point: 1,315 feet
Trail type: Gated logging road, through clear-cuts
Avalanche potential: None
Difficulty level: Moderate
Maps: USGS Lake Whatcom and USGS Alger (7.5' series)

The Hike

The "Alp" is only a thousand-foot blip on the landscape—but such a prominent one. From north or south, look off to the northeast as you exit at Alger, and there it is, just sitting there looking like an inverted thimble.

And what a serendipitous surprise in the view department!

Getting There

Take Interstate 5 Exit 240, Alger, and go east 0.8 mile to an intersection with Old Highway 99. Continue across, now on Alger–Cain Lake Road, but don't go heavy on the gas pedal. In a quarter mile park on wide turnouts before an easily noticed concrete bridge over unsigned Silver Creek. Walk back 150 feet toward Old 99 and find a yellow-gated dirt road on the right (north) side of Alger–Cain Lake Road.

The Trail

The road is the route to the summit. Although there are several possible left turns along the way, the choice is never difficult. Always stay right and always go up. In season, note the rich scent of pale lemon-colored flowers of red elderberry. Farther up grows an abundance of red flowering currant.

One mile into the walk, at 800 feet elevation, you encounter a designer-quality S-turn that puts you onto the back of a knife-edge ridge, which makes a natural ramp for easing the road onto the thimble. At **1.4** miles drop to a connecting saddle at 950 feet, about two-thirds of the way up.

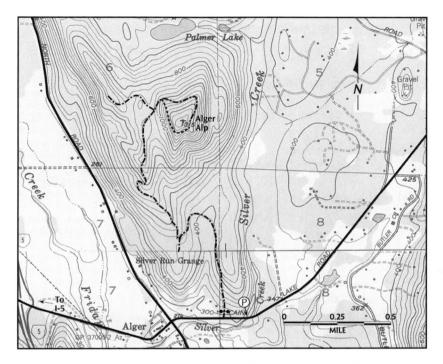

The stretch of road ahead gives the best views off the north side of the Alp. From the saddle the road climbs pretty much east for a while. Where it curves sharply south at **1.6** miles (1,060 feet), stop on a wide shoulder to admire the arc of lakes below. From west to east they are Samish, Squires, Palmer, Cain, Reed, and Whatcom, all pearls embedded in woodland green.

Go up, for the top is quite near, and the 360-degree view calls loudly. In the west watch motorized midgets crawl the I-5 trace, some with segmented bodies and eighteen legs. Due west, beyond the freeway, sits Blanchard Mountain, due east is Anderson, while Cultus (or Fire Mountain) rises in the southeast (130 degrees).

Northward, the extreme south end of Lookout Mountain climbs from the shores of Palmer and Squires Lakes. And to the south? A vast panorama of hills and farms and towns to Mount Vernon and beyond.

24 | SKAGIT COUNTY
Anderson Mountain

🥾🥾🥾🥾

Distance:	2.9 miles round-trip
Time:	1.5 to 3 hours
Starting elevation:	3,000 feet
High point:	3,364 feet
Trail type:	Blocked forest roads to summit ridge
Avalanche potential:	None
Difficulty level:	Easy
Maps:	USGS Lake Whatcom and USGS Alger (7.5' series)

The Hike

A nice thing about Anderson Mountain is the low ratio of energy output to view gain. A good dirt road, rarely if ever gated, goes to within a mile of the top. There is a geological oddity on the summit as well, mere spice for seasoning those gourmet views.

It is a terrific sunset hike, too, and flashlight or moonlight will do nicely when coming down.

Getting There

From the south, take Interstate 5 Exit 230, Cook Road, and start east. Almost immediately, turn left (north) onto Pacific Highway. In 6.2 miles, turn right (east) on Parson Creek Road.

From the north, take I-5 Exit 240, Alger, and go left (east) 0.8 mile to Pacific Highway. Turn right (south) for another mile to Parson Creek Road, 1.8 miles from I-5, and turn left (east).

From either direction, reset your odometer at Parson Creek Road. In 0.4 mile, turn left (north) on Butler Creek Road, then right (east) on Echo Hill Road at 0.5 mile. The last turn, at 1.2 miles from Pacific Highway, is a left (north) on Skaarup Road. Skaarup soon becomes Anderson Mountain Road without any more turns.

The 8.0-mile mark brings you to a barely perceptible height of land. The road glides gently downhill to a four-way intersection 8.4 miles from Pacific

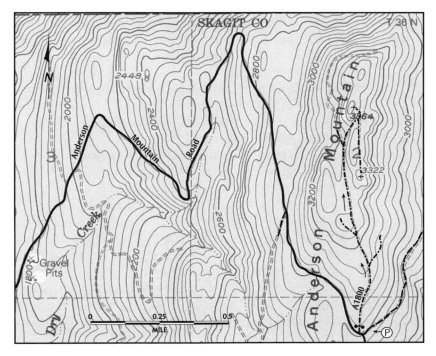

Highway. Park there. The walking route is north up a deeply bermed road signed for Road A-1800.

The Trail

The old road rises gently to the north, encountering a Y at **0.2** mile. Go left and up. Take the right fork of a second Y at **0.5** mile. Soon note a beautiful carpet of moss at the right side of the roadway, and note also the dirt-bike tire print slashed through it. One more turn at the **0.8**-mile point brings the third and last Y. Take the right fork and climb once more, dodging alder saplings for a tenth of a mile. You soon arrive at a saddle on Anderson Mountain's ridge. Here, **0.9** mile, the road swings sharply to the south and to wonderful views north, east, and south.

But hold on. Anderson's true summit is 0.2 mile round-trip northward on a steep-sided tuft of tree-covered rock. To get there, look for a slight opening in the young trees on the north side of the road bend in the saddle. Push through the pearly everlasting and fireweed stalks to a low, 6-foot-wide pile of rotting, silvery wood. Do not confuse the small pile with a larger one to its right (or east). On the far side of the wood pile is the start of a short, limb-cut, debris-dragged "trail" most of the way up the mound. A pair of ropes has been placed to help with footing on the loose soil, but the ascent is not dangerous even without the ropes.

At the top of the second rope, look right (east) for the always magnificent visage of Mount Baker, flanked by the chocolate glow of the entire Twin Sisters Range. Take a deep breath, then go left on little footpaths to the summit, and a rocky, very picturesque overlook at 3,364 feet.

A sweeping view encompasses Mount Washington at the south end of the Olympics to Hurricane Ridge in the north. To the southwest along a bearing of 233 degrees, pick out the two oil refineries on March Point near Anacortes as well as the ubiquitous dome of Mount Erie. Islands are everywhere.

Down in the valley, close-in and due west (270 degrees), sits the mighty Alger Alp (Hike 23), and over its head on the same line is Blanchard Mountain, sporting the Oyster Dome (Hike 19). The dome, a 300-foot cliff, is visible on the mountain's north skyline. Slightly north of due west, directly over Chuckanut Mountain's midpoint (277 degrees), lie Lummi Island and Peak, then the rock ramparts of Mount Constitution (Hike 15) on Orcas Island. Off Orcas's north coast you can see clear to Vancouver Island and British Columbia's Gulf Islands.

Back down in the saddle, and on the east side of the big bend along the now ridge-top road, walk out onto a log landing for vistas north and south. The view is up and down the SR 9 valley. Southward, if it is visible, is Mount Rainier, 130 air miles away, the ice cream sundae in the sky.

Back on the road, now **1.2** miles into the hike, walk the quarter mile south to its end and more great views. The turnaround is the **1.45**-mile mark. Cultus Mountain (Hike 27), to the extreme southeast, is at 160 degrees, and at its foot is the lush Skagit River Valley.

And those geological oddities? Peer down from the extreme east edge of the graveled turnaround at road's end and find a long trench with a rock rib forming its outer rim. There are more of these in the woods to the west. One can safely walk down into them.

Anderson Mountain is composed of loose soil and weak phyllite rock. Geologists theorize that once the vast glacial ice melted away, the unsupported sides of the landform bulged outward, leading to the splitting evident along its crest. This glacial process and end result were much like the wearing and subsequent removal of a girdle: Sagging is sure to result.

25 Big Rock

Distance:	0.9 mile round-trip
Time:	1.25 hours
Starting elevation:	100 feet
High point:	529 feet
Trail type:	Four-wheel-drive roads and open ledge walking
Avalanche potential:	None
Difficulty level:	Strenuous, steep and slippery with fall hazards
Map:	USGS Mount Vernon (7.5' series)

The valley view of State Route 9, looking south from the summit of Big Rock.

The Hike

Big Rock demands big respect. It is no place for irresponsible adults or for unmanageable children. The top 200 vertical feet of its ascent are on exposed rock that is very slippery when wet. Still, it is a hike, not a rock climb. There are safe ways to the summit, but the possibility of long falls is definitely there.

Despite its diminutive proportions, this rock gets a lot of respect in the view department, too.

Getting There

Drive Interstate 5 to Exit 227, College Parkway, in Mount Vernon. Go east 3.6 miles to State Route 9 and turn right (south). At 4.0 miles, turn around and park on the northbound shoulder.

The Trail

There are no signs, but a muddy four-wheel-drive road angling southward off the west side of the highway is the start. It is steep from the 10-foot point to the top.

In a tad more than a tenth of a mile, already at 240 feet, turn right on another dirt road. Go up on short switchbacks, churned into muddy ruts by adult power toys, to 320 feet. The road becomes trail, but it is only a connector to a third road segment. Go right again. When that, too, narrows to become a trail, Big Rock looms ahead.

Out of the trees and at the base of the rock, the trail passes beneath a leaning log, then angles upward in diagonal cracks in bedrock. Boot scuffs and mudprints point the way. The safest route makes one long diagonal leg generally northwest to some shrubs, then one more long leg to the east and northeast to the summit.

There is at least an acre of safe, bouldery ground on top, but the transition to vertical is sudden on all sides. Make note of the start of the safe descent route.

Views are everywhere, but start by looking at the summit plateau itself. This old rock is here because that old glacier couldn't knock it down. Scars on the rock testify that it tried. Embedded in the rock is a plaque proclaiming the summit area to be Dr. Richard M. Hoag Memorial Park, and a fitting monument it is.

In the north, views are blocked by trees, but by moving to a safe stance on the east edge you get back much of the missing band. Due north is Anderson

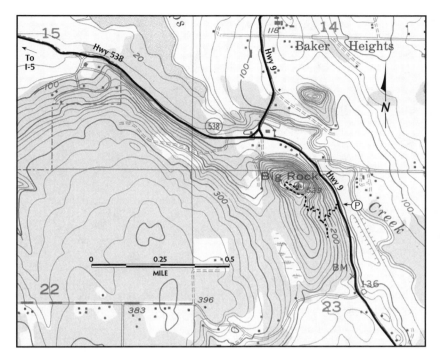

Mountain (Hike 24); beside it and a bit more east is massive Lyman Hill. Mount Baker, of course, needs no bearing.

Cultus Mountain is about due east, but what's that big bite out of its side? Read about getting up there (Hike 27) and get one version of what "they" think happened.

Move around the summit. In the west, the view is down to the flatlands of the Skagit Delta. Big Lake is southeast on a bearing of 147 degrees. Along with Big Lake and Big Rock, there is Little Mountain (Hike 26), southwest at 228 degrees. The day is young; why not do it next?

26 Little Mountain

Distance:	3.0 miles round-trip
Time:	2 hours
Starting elevation:	60 feet
High point:	980 feet
Trail type:	Forest trails to observation area
Avalanche potential:	None
Difficulty level:	Strenuous
Map:	USGS Mount Vernon (7.5' series)

The Hike

This "little" mountain is a big adversary.

That sounds like something a person would say of an opponent he or she had just beaten, but not by much. We're toying around here, but the message is straight. Do not underestimate this one because of its name. The only thing little about this mountain is the amount of parking room at the trailhead. There really isn't any.

Getting There

Drive Interstate 5 to East Hickox Road, Exit 224, in south Mount Vernon. On the end of the overpass, jog left (north) on Cedardale, the outer road, for a couple of blocks, then turn right (east) onto East Hickox Road for 1.0 mile. On the left (north) side of the road, find mailbox 1819, then a long gravel driveway in a corridor of trees. To the right of the driveway is the trailhead.

The box and the drive, as well as much of the land bearing the first half mile of trail, belong to Dr. and Mrs. Fred Darvill. Fred is a mountain man, a man of medicine, and he's been a writer of hiking guidebooks for many years. Display your guest manners, please. The one request the Darvills have is that folks be down before dark.

About the parking—sadly, one must either jam a vehicle onto the narrow shoulder (and hope for the benevolence of the MVPD) or park a half mile farther east and walk to the trailhead.

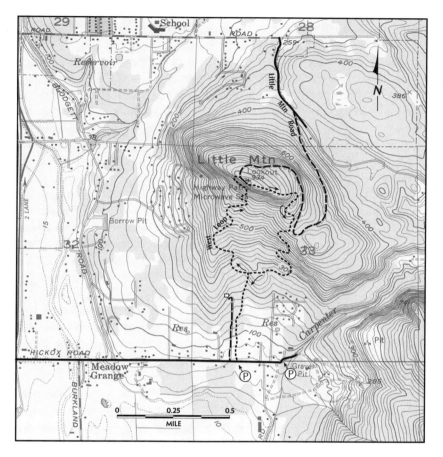

The Trail

The route parallels the long driveway, then starts up the lower flank of the mountain. The park boundary is reached at **0.6** mile. At **0.7** mile the trail splits, with the left fork becoming the West Loop Trail, and the right, though it is not signed as such, being the normal summit route. The distance to the top is just under a mile either way.

With loop trails, it often makes little difference which way one goes, but it makes a good deal of difference on Little Mountain. Both ways are steep, but up near the top of the West Loop Trail, the terrain becomes steep in the extreme with fewer trees to grab. It's not a rock climb, though, and any falls along its path will be just slips and slides. The point to be made is that if you choose to do the West Loop Trail at all, do it on the way up.

We'd have gone left even if warned. The trail drops slightly to the west before rising moderately and swinging more to the north. It then steepens and trends northeasterly to avoid a deep gully on the left. The main mass of the summit knob looms ahead. At **1.3** miles bypass a trail coming in from the left with green blazes. Soon, the designation "steep" takes on new meaning, but just as soon, it is nearly over. Fling your body over the final lip at **1.4** miles and pause for breath. (Actually, you will probably have remained upright the entire way.)

Across the final 0.1 mile on horizontal ground is a covered observation platform and a fenced walkway along the precipice. In the extreme south of the view are Devil's and Scott Mountains, both hacked upon unmercifully by *Homo termitus*, a resistant, wood-devouring species. Blocked by very little, except weather and a little curvature of Mother Earth, is Mount Rainier.

Don't use your compass near the fence or in the observation shelter: too much steel. Fifteen or twenty feet away should be okay.

The Skagit Delta takes over to the west. See the winding waterway split into a downstream Y, much like a trail. Out over the fast track of I-5 are the river towns of Conway and La Conner. On the sound, most of the visible island property is on very linear Whidbey. And, of course, ignore that horizon full of Olympic Mountains.

Going down is definitely an anticlimax, but heck, you gotta do it. Walk eastward along the view fence to pick up the trail behind the chain-link barrier around the two tall antennas. The path goes flat briefly along the rim, then starts downward in varying degrees of moderate and steep. There are several unsigned side routes on the descent, but all gravitate to the main trail.

For a time the ascent road is on the left, then the gradient slacks off. When a clear-cut appears downhill and left of the trail, the completion of the loop is not far off. From the junction with the West Loop Trail, go left (south) just three-quarters of a mile to the car, assuming it hasn't been towed.

27 SKAGIT COUNTY
Cultus Mountain

🥾🥾🥾🥾

Distance:	12.2 or 14.6 miles round-trip
Time:	7 or 9 hours
Starting elevation:	765 feet
High point:	3,997 feet
Trail type:	Gated forest roads leading to summit trail
Avalanche potential:	Slight, last half mile
Difficulty level:	Moderate, occasionally strenuous
Map:	USGS Sedro Woolley South (7.5' series)

The Hike

Cultus, also known as Fire Mountain, is a 4,000-footer (almost) and is just 10 air miles from Interstate 5. With that advantage its view opportunities range over half (well, maybe only a third) of the known world. And stir this intangible into the mix: Something very geologically mysterious happened up there.

On the mountain's southwestern shoulder, and visible from all over the valley, is a great cavity called the Big Hole. With such a cataclysmic tear in the firma, one could well expect to find a roughly equal volume of rock and earth somewhere below, and indeed there is. Most of it, however, is found a mile and a half away at a place called (what else?) Devil's Garden.

How did that happen? Popular guesses center around a steam explosion or an otherwise-triggered landslide that fell during the close of the last ice age. Moving, then melting, ice could have been the vehicle.

Planning for Cultus requires careful attention to snow levels and possibly carrying snowshoes.

Getting There

From the south, take Interstate 5 Mount Vernon Exit 277, College Way, also named State Route 538 East. Drive east 3.6 miles to a junction with SR 9. Turn left (north) to the 7.0-mile point, just north of the town of Clear Lake. Turn right (east) on Old Day Creek Road, and at 10.3 miles turn right (south) on Jan-icke Road.

Just after crossing beneath power lines at 11.4 miles, then trading pavement for a graveled road surface, park at a gated logging road on the left (east) in a clear-cut, 11.6 miles from I-5. The correct road, the walking route, doubles back sharply to the north in contrast to the southerly approach while on Janicke Road.

The Trail

First an explanation: The 12.2 or 14.6 miles round-trip figures involve a choice between an alternative off-trail shortcut and a side trip for super views, both explained where appropriate.

From the trailhead, hike past the gate for about 1.5 miles to the northeast on level to gently rising gravel roadway, make a hairpin turn back to the southeast, continue climbing steadily, and walk a second mile. All of the terrain so far is clear-cut. The forest road flattens out as it enters mature timber. Keep going. In another mile, **3.5** miles from the gate, the route breaks out once again into the upper reaches of a vast clear-cut.

At **3.7** miles the road reaches a Y. The intersection may not be on the topo you are using. The better-looking but ill-advised choice, the right fork, starts losing elevation (oh, horrors) at a meaningful rate. Take the left fork, a much diminished roadway, and soon head back into the timber again.

After nearly a half mile of easy walking from the Y, ignoring a couple of old roads leading left, the roadway vanishes at an old washout at Mundt Creek (**4.1** miles total).

Thanks to the hard work of some local off-road bikers, a bypass trail goes downstream around the chasm, then over a footbridge to rejoin the road.

At **4.3** miles from the trailhead (1,960 feet) reach Key Junction, a well-marked Y draped with yards of surveyor's tape and sporting signs with arrows pointing the way.

Head upward on the left fork, the way choked with salmonberry and young alders for a time. Notice also the steepening grade. On the way, you encounter a serious washout of the old road, but it soon gets back to good going.

It is more than a 2.0-mile chug from Key Junction to Upper Junction. There, at 3,300 feet, and **6.4** miles from Janicke Road, the way tees into obviously driveable logging road once more.

Sense the summit! Turn right (south) at the T, and climb some more for a strong quarter mile. As the driveable road levels out, look for an opening on the left in thinning tree cover. It looks to have once been a road segment heading southeast but is now the beginning of the summit trail. It is steadily

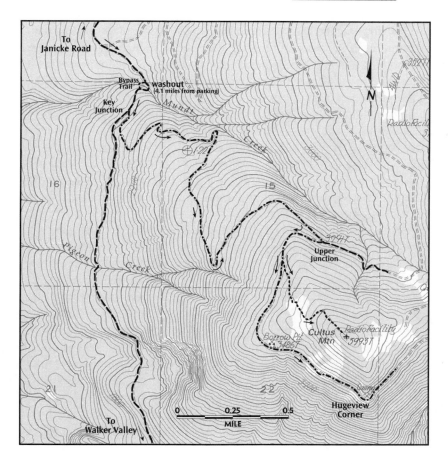

To
Janicke Road

Bypass
Trail   washout
Key   (4.1 miles from parking)
Junction

Mundt

Creek

N

16

15

Pigeon

Creek

Upper
Junction

Borrow Pit   Cultus   Radio Fac(lit)
Mtn

Hugeview
Corner

To
Walker Valley

0   0.25   0.5
MILE

upward now, but go with new vigor. It is only 0.6 mile more, **7.3** miles in all, to the top.

There is no 360-degree sweep from Cultus, but impressive segments of the panorama are easily obtained by moving around the top, a summit that has been royally scalped to make space for communications equipment.

Look north over Mundt Peak, Cultus Mountain's companion summit, and drink in Baker and the Twin Sisters in their erminesque robes. Gaze west over the sound country and to the Olympic Mountains as far as the auto haze permits. The view south is restricted, but read on for an astounding remedy for the problem, no chain saw involved.

Back down where the trail rejoins the good logging road, go left (south) instead of back toward your car. Walk a flattish 1.0 mile south past a quarry, then southeast to another one, where the road swings back to the northeast, but go no farther. This is well-named Hugeview Corner, and now it is cricket to talk of "sweeping."

Do the 270-degree view ramble from Sahale Peak in the east (85 degrees), to Glacier Peak, Whitehorse Mountain, and the spires of Three Fingers, the latter three all southeast. Roll your eyeballs south over the Stillaguamish country to the great ice cream sundae called Mount Rainier.

Don't stop there. Need we point out the Olympic Mountains? And in the glistening sound before them, a jillion islands, all the way up to British Columbia's Vancouver Island.

Making use of the promised alternative off-trail shortcut is an easy way to justify adding that 2.0-mile hike out to Hugeview. It's a bit rough but it chops 2.4 miles off the round-trip.

Back at the trailhead, go around the gate and head up as described. In 0.4 mile, though, look for an essentially nondriveable and overgrown road on the right (east) and follow it. The road curves southeast, back toward mature trees. It never enters them but stays in the clear-cut, swinging around to trend north.

In a second 0.4 mile, a total of 0.8 from the gate, notice the only stand of thirty or so mature trees in the clear-cut to the left (west). On the right (east) side of the road at that point stands fully grown forest. Also on the right is a really large boulder, and just before the boulder is a small tree sporting orange metal blazes, the start of the easy bushwhack.

The blazes are only in place for a hundred yards or so, but they really are not necessary. (There are some on the other end, too.) The shortcut goes due east just inside the mature trees. Out to the left (north) all is recent clear-cut. Follow along inside the forest for about a half mile, picking up remnants of boot tracks here and there, until the route comes out on the road above. A little scuffling with deadfall, and with very little brush, has cut off 1.2 miles, one way, on the trip to the top.

Those are "Hugeview" miles.

SKAGIT COUNTY

28 Frailey Mountain

Distance:	8.8 miles round-trip
Time:	5.5 hours
Starting elevation:	1,100 feet
High point:	2,666 feet
Trail type:	Gated forest roads to summit
Avalanche potential:	Slight
Difficulty level:	Easy to strenuous, little in between
Maps:	USGS Stimson Hill and USGS Oso (7.5' series)

The Hike

Looking at Frailey Mountain from nearby summits, it looks as if some geological think-tankers decided to plunk down a 12-mile-long hoagie in order to keep Lake Cavanaugh from emptying into the North Fork Stillaguamish. It didn't work, but the "hoagie" is still there, and while looking a bit raked over by the fiber harvesters, it is a nice place to go for seldom-seen perspectives on the North Fork valley.

Getting There

Leave Interstate 5 at Exit 208, Sylvana-Arlington, and drive east on State Route 530 to milepost 32.8 in Oso. Turn left (north) onto Lake Cavanaugh Road, noting or resetting your odometer at the turn. Views from the road of the Stillaguamish Valley are phenomenal. In 3.5 miles, on a sharp switchback, park at a gated road leading west.

The Trail

Ten minutes from the gate, ignore a right fork and climb west on ORV-usable old road. At **1.1** miles, 1,820 feet, it tees into a good gravel road. The route is unspeakably downhill to the left for 400 vertical feet from the intersection.

It takes a bit over a half mile to bottom out the dreadful descent, then, at 1,440 feet and the **1.6**-mile mark, go right at a Y that leads upward with an impersonal vengeance.

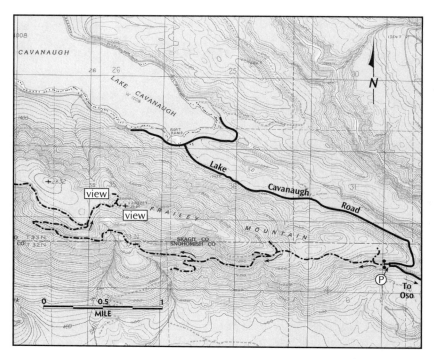

At 1,760 feet, **2.0** miles from Lake Cavanaugh Road, a deeply trenched spur road leads leftward to a nearby log landing with excellent sights. The 2,060-foot elevation brings with it a 1.0-mile breather straight west and almost flat, with view after view downriver. The climbing renews with vigor, and, in another half mile, leads to a milestone saddle at 2,480 feet, **3.9** miles from the trailhead.

The saddle is on the main ridge of the mountain, while the lookout site is a half mile away on a subridge to the northeast. Ignore a road entering from the left. Continue north, losing 40 vertical feet but gaining some nice views to the east.

At last reach the top, 2,666 feet and as high as one can get on Frailey. Unfortunately for the esthetics, the place is also outfitted with a noisy and smelly generator that runs the generic summit communications equipment. Take shallow breaths, and stay upwind.

North and east, trees block all of that sweeping approach-road panorama, but look west for grin-bringing gapes out over Arlington and Puget Sound, and on into the Olympics. At 150 degrees southeast, looking truly imposing, rises Mount Pilchuck.

In spite of the tree cover there is an unexpected bonus for views northward. Start down the road, but almost immediately find a rudimentary trail on the right (north) not more than a hundred steps from the tower. Trundle down the easily discernible way 0.1 mile to a view stump on a salal-covered precipice, and look into Lake Cavanaugh 1,600 feet below. The view is northwesterly into a rectangular bay that contains the outlet for the lake. Look beyond that to the nearly vertical contours of 2,486-foot Bald Mountain, a landform so unique you may think someone has stolen Devil's Tower from Wyoming.

Perhaps, as you gaze, a red-tailed hawk will rise up whisper-winged on thermals and into your space as it did ours. It is always time out for such wildlife moments.

29 Gee Point

Distance:	3.0 miles round-trip
Time:	3 hours
Starting elevation:	4,400 feet
High point:	4,974 feet
Trail type:	Rough trail in forest to summit
Avalanche potential:	Caution advised
Difficulty level:	Moderate to strenuous
Maps:	Green Trails Oso No. 77 or USGS Gee Point (7.5' series)

The Hike

Gee (as in gee whiz) Point is simply a must-do, but it may be pushing the concept of snowy-season hikes. Its trailhead is at 4,400 feet, and the area is close to the weather-making influence of bigger mountains. The summit, once the site of a fire lookout, is a craggy and blunt-topped cone barely 25 feet across.

The fact is, the Gee experience is too fantastic to leave out because of a few possible snags. Do it early or do it late in the snowy season, but by all means, do it!

Getting There

Drive Interstate 5 to Burlington Exit 230. Go east on State Route 20 to milepost 88.2 on the western edge of Concrete. Reset your odometer. Turn right (south) on Concrete–Sauk Valley Road and cross the Skagit River in 1.0 mile. At the south end of the bridge turn left (east) still on the Concrete–Sauk Valley Road to Darrington.

At 9.9 miles from SR 20 turn right (southeast) on Finney Creek Road, a paved, single-lane logging road with turnouts. Watch yourself, for the pavement seems to lull folks into driving much too fast. Since the route also has mile markers, watch for MP 10 (nice veil-type waterfall there), then check off 0.6 mile more to a gravel road right (west).

Set your odometer to 0.0 once more, then take the right turn. At 2.0 miles up (2,480 feet), go right again at a Y. At 5.5 miles and another Y, take the left fork, following it to its end at 4,400 feet and 7.1 miles from Finney Creek

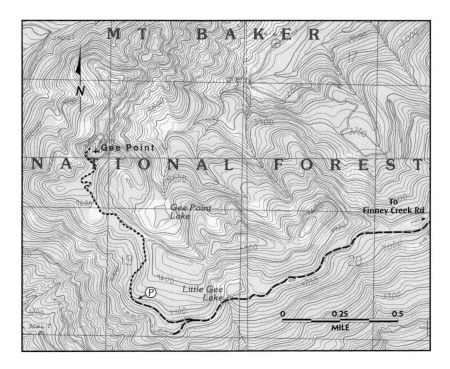

Road. Park. Scenery from the high road is spectacular and only gets better on the mountain.

The Trail

The road to the trailhead was once driveable 0.2 mile beyond the parking area but is now blocked. Walk its course to the end of recognizable old road. From that point, a barely discernible path leads right and off into the grasses and brush. The rest of the route to the summit is stump-dodging, brush-grabbingly satisfying. Except for the beginning, you won't have to wonder where the path is, but under some conditions, such as two or three inches of new snow, it could be a different story.

At 4,480 feet the route flattens and becomes more trail-like for a time. It then skirts the east edge of a gorgeous meadow. At **1.1** miles (4,700 feet) you reach a clearing and the site of an almost totally vanished cabin. Likely, it was living quarters for the lookout person over the years.

From the cabin clearing, the same sparse trail you have been on goes hard left and climbs upward on or just left of a small talus slope. The path is easily relocated at the top where it goes right, crossing a spiny connecting ridge. Straight ahead is a scary-looking rock wall, the base of Gee Point's summit cone.

At the wall the route goes left and calls for a little caution. (It's not exposed, just rough.) After another 150 vertical feet of sidehill gouging and huckleberry holds, the spectacular summit is gained.

You may literally twirl a few times looking for a place to begin taking in the views. They start with three volcanoes: Baker, Rainier, and Glacier Peak in the east and southeast, followed by the Twin Sisters Range due north, with its coating of hot-chocolate brown. From the Pickets in the northeast to Mount Rainier due south, you can scan the entire North Cascades skyline.

To the west are the distant misty isles of Puget Sound and their wondrous background curtain of Olympic peaks. Northwest from there sit the San Juans, as well as Canada's equivalent, the Gulf Islands.

On Gee's breathtaking point, a little twirling is very understandable.

30 North Mountain

Distance:	2.6 miles round-trip from the gate (with the gate at elevation 3,360 feet, the walking portion could be much longer than 2.6 miles round-trip in the snowy season)
Time:	2.5 hours
Starting elevation:	3,360 feet
High point:	3,824 feet
Trail type:	Gated forest roads
Avalanche potential:	Slight
Difficulty level:	Easy to moderate
Map:	Green Trails Darrington No. 78

A lookout atop North Mountain.

The Hike

Looming over the southeast side of the town of Darrington is magnificent Whitehorse Mountain, but anything that big and gorgeous can only be of scenic value to the inhabitants. It is left to North Mountain to be the town overseer as well as watchdog for three major river valleys, and it sports a working and climbable lookout tower.

But here is the real significance of North Mountain's positioning. Where it arrests its plunge to equilibrium with the flat plane of Darrington, two major rivers are *less than 3.0 miles* apart. Within that span, each river crosses the 500-foot contour line on its way to destiny, all the while with little more than 100 feet of topographical rise in the land separating the two. The crux of this little wowie is this: The Sauk is rushing *north* while the Stillaguamish races *south*.

Getting There

Drive State Route 530 east from Interstate 5 Exit 208. Right after milepost 49, on the east edge of Darrington, swing left (north) with SR 530. Pass the Darrington Ranger District Office on the left. At MP 50.1, turn left (west) onto North Fork Stillaguamish Road, signed Forest Road 28. It is also signed for North Mountain Lookout, 14 miles. There is not much more meaningful signage, so reset your odometer at the turn and watch it carefully.

Just 2.0 miles up, great views are already opening across the wide valley. But, this is no river valley below. It is that 3.0-mile-wide separation between the Stilly and the Sauk you see.

At 3.0 miles the pavement ends as the road splits. Forest Road 28 continues left and down to the river. Take the right fork. It is FR 2810, which keeps this same number nearly all the way to the top. A sort of T appears at 6.7 miles and FR 2810 leads right. Stay with it as it climbs back to the south. Five more of these north-south reversals occur before you reach the gate. At 8.3 miles (2,380 feet), ignore a road to the right. At 9.5 miles ignore a side road left (east) and keep chugging.

At 12.4 miles from SR 530 (3,360 feet), park at a gate, whether open or not. Appreciation for the total setting demands walking from here—and besides, the top is an easy 1.3 miles away.

The Trail

Walk the road, enjoying views west and northwest much of the way. At **1.0** mile, where FR 2810 continues northeasterly, go right with the more traveled

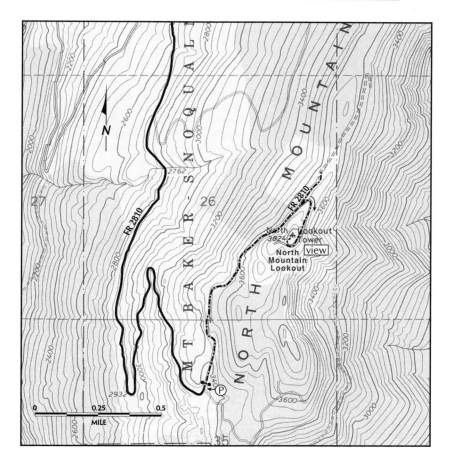

way as it switches sharply southward. The route also asserts itself more steeply for the first and only time. The summit, with its accessible tower, is reached **1.3** miles from the gate.

What can one say of views that have been great from the bottom up? Wider, more distant, and 360 degrees worth of them, that's what. One cannot get them all from ground level, so it's off to the tower with you.

Mount Higgins is a great hike but a summer event only. Its summit is located nearly due west at 267 degrees. The dome to the right of Higgins is Round Mountain. An end-on view of the entire Twin Sisters Range, northwest at 328 degrees, makes it look like only two peaks, but there are a full dozen in a line, many of them 5,000-footers.

Mount Baker and the Black Buttes need no introduction, and certainly no compass bearing: They are a mighty combo to see. Mount Shuksan, so dwarfed and often so hidden by Baker, sits perfectly astride the 0-degree mark looking from North Mountain. Shuksan has a daggerlike summit thrust that is a daunting sight even from this distance but downright intimidating when approached on snowfields leading up to it. To the northeast lie the numerous needles of the Picket Range. Southeast, 122 degrees, is Glacier Peak. To its right is a trio of very sheer and very cold-looking spires named Whitechuck, Pugh, Sloan, and Bedal.

The deep valley appearing to lie between Pugh and Bedal is that of the Sauk River. It has its headwaters in the glaciers above Monte Cristo, then rushes past Darrington to meld with the Skagit.

Your melding is with a wheeled conveyance, and as always, after sniffing the air of the mountain world, you are likely a bit more humble than when you came up.

Deception Pass State Park

Could it be that a single 4,000-acre park has everything? Deception Pass State Park comes awfully close.

Within its boundaries, spanning parts of two major islands, lie a pair of good-size freshwater lakes surrounded by topography only recently given up, in geological terms, by glacial ice. In that extremely rugged terrain are a half dozen or so equally rough minimountains, from whose summits both the Cascade and Olympic Mountains can be seen. There are magnificent old-growth forests, a mile-long beach with natural sand dunes, and the whole place is festooned with some 12 to 15 miles of Puget Sound shoreline.

And the bridge! Everyone brings visitors from other areas to see the awesome span, to walk its length, to feel it sing in the wind, and to *ooo* and *ahh* with the scads of other visitors. Now you can be the one to break it to them all, for Deception Pass Bridge is two bridges, not one, and it crosses two water passages as well.

Tidepools, swirling currents, bald eagles, and wildflowers—all are here, along with days of fine hiking. There are two campgrounds, a boat launch, and an underwater park, too. Come any season, but the only relative seclusion will be found in December and January. This is also the best time from another point of view, for in those two months other snowy-season hikes are apt to be, well, a little *too* snowy.

Getting There

The park's great trails divide nicely into four enjoyable days. Following are the general directions for getting to the area. Each hike description includes the directions to its own trailhead.

From the south, drive Interstate 5 to Exit 189 and go west to Mukilteo. Ferry across to Clinton on the Whidbey Island side and drive State Route 525 north to its intersection with SR 20. Continue north on SR 20 to various Deception Pass Park entrances and interest points from milepost 40.8 to MP 42.8.

From the north, take I-5 Exit 230 in Burlington and drive SR 20 all the way to MP 42.8 and the first of the park's entrances.

31 N. & W. Beach & Dunes

Distance:	3.0 to 5.0 miles total
Time:	3 to 5 hours
Starting elevation:	10 feet
High point:	40 feet
Trail type:	Various: beaches and dune forest
Avalanche potential:	None
Difficulty level:	Easy
Map:	USGS Deception Pass (7.5' series)

The Hike

West Beach and North Beach are different as day and night from one another. About the only thing they have in common is saltwater. Sounds untrue? After all, they are in the same park, and, as they meet at West Point, the two beaches form a contiguous stretch of the same coastline!

The Ridge Dune at West Beach.

West Beach runs north and south and is a great deal like Pacific beaches. Its west view, if one could see that far, is practically out to Neah Bay. Little wonder there is real surf here, for there is little to break the winds off the Pacific. The same winds give rise to the unique sand dunes of West Beach.

North Beach forms the south shore of Deception Pass and so swings abruptly east from the rocky protrusion of West Point. Though the waters of the pass boil with conflicting currents and eddies, the beach itself is sheltered from south winds by the dense forest at its back.

Getting There

See the Deception Pass State Park introduction (pages 95–96) for directions to the area.

At milepost 41.3 of State Route 20, turn west into the park's Whidbey Island entrance, which is signed for Cranberry Lake, West Beach, West Point, and North Beach. Immediately inside the gate a right turn goes to North Beach, but keep going to West Point. Park in the large area provided and focus left (south) on West Beach first.

The Trail

The watchword for West Beach, except for the dunes, is to wander at will. Stay on marked trails in the dunes; there is too much fragile landscaping for running about. Abundant ecological signage along the dunes trail makes the dunes' continuing evolution come alive. On windy days they build and move right before the eyes. Run all you wish along West Beach itself. It goes for miles, in and out of the park.

For the dune walk, trudge south through the parking lot and past the restroom building. The paved trail, 0.7 mile in length, also a wheelchair-accommodating loop, is just beyond.

For the eco-switch to North Beach; West Point itself must be dealt with, for it is a buttress of rock that juts into the channel. There are trails inland around it, starting at the extreme northeast end of the parking area, or scramble over the rocks like so many others. Once on the sand, it's possible to walk the beach for a mile, with a couple of detours along the way involving rocks and ledges. The first, a nameless bedrock mass, is scootable on sand at low water, but the other, Gun Point, a small but mighty headland nearer the bridge, is more safely bypassed on its inland side.

After exploring the beach east of Gun Point, the return to West Point may be made the same way or, for a change of pace, back through the marvelous

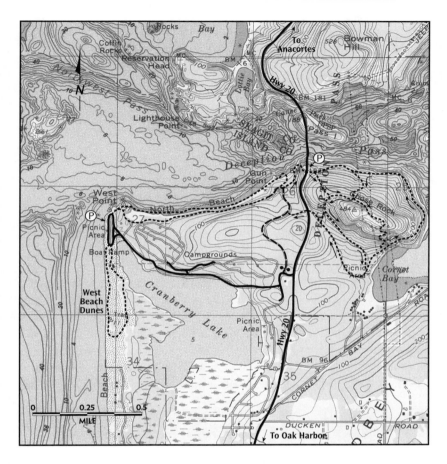

forest. Find the trail by following the service road west from the parking area in the trees behind Gun Point. It parallels the beach and ends at the campfire amphitheater 150 feet or so from the rocks of West Point.

32 Rosario Head

🥾🥾🥾🥾🥾

Distance:	3.2 to 5.2 miles round-trip
Time:	3 to 6 hours
Starting elevation:	20 feet
High point:	120 feet
Trail type:	Forests and bluffs
Avalanche potential:	None
Difficulty level:	Easy, moderate, some strenuous
Map:	USGS Deception Pass (7.5' series)

The Hike

Speaking poetically, this hike is a golden chain strung with gems. To stroll the chain by itself is a three-mile walk, but to enjoy it with all of its precious stones adds two more miles.

The "chain" portion of the route, 3.2 miles round-trip, runs along the shoreline and connects two ridges with two beaches. The "gems" are two headlands attached to the shoreline trail by slender causeways of sand and earth. Adding in the headland walks brings the total miles to 5.2. (The

On the trail to Canoe Pass.

mileage count assumes the headlands will be bypassed on the return trip.) Five-plus miles is not a long hike, but this one has many ups and downs and numerous side trail possibilities.

Getting There

See the Deception Pass State Park introduction (pages 95–96) for directions to the area.

At milepost 42.8 on State Route 20, directly at the south end of Pass Lake, turn west into the park, signed for Bowman Bay and Rosario Beach. An immediate left goes to Bowman Bay. Go past it on Rosario Road for 0.6 mile to a left (west) turn signed for Rosario Beach. You may park at the beach if the gate is open. If it isn't, parking at the gate adds only a couple of hundred feet to the hike.

The Trail

From the parking area, follow the graveled path left and past the group picnic shelter. Beyond the shelter follow the path right (west) to the 0.4-mile loop out around Rosario Head. (To bypass the head, walk left along the water for the trail to Bowman Bay.)

Walk across the isthmus, with driftlogs on the Rosario Beach side and with a more sheltered beach and a public moorage on the other. Just before the headland is an interesting cedar carving of the Fish Maiden, a woman who, according to Native American legend, became a fish and went to live in the sea. The sculpture shows different women, in different dress, on either side of the figure.

Beyond, the trail splits to make the loop. Go either way. The seaward half of the head is treeless, grassy bedrock, and views are impressive. Look due south between Deception Island and the large mass of Reservation Head. The view is of West Point, then down along the park's dunes and beaches to the naval air station and beyond. Inland from Reservation Head is the huge public fishing pier on the beach at Bowman Bay.

Off the headland and past the Fish Maiden is the **0.5**-mile point of the walk. No trail shows on the lawn, but walk its edge southeasterly along the shore to pick up a trail. It climbs over rugged and sometimes sheer hillside above the bay, with great views. Drop to a campground and to the beach at Bowman Bay.

Walk south beyond the huge public pier at **1.3** miles, once part of a salmon rearing project. Pick up trail again as it crosses a wetland and runs smack into the side of the next ridge to cross. Out to the right is Reservation Head, and past the insurmountable waterside cliff you will see the grass and sand strip that links the head to the main island. Kick into low, and climb the switchbacks to more excellent viewing from up on the hump. Starting down, ignore a trail left, and drop to the obvious beginning of the Reservation Head Loop Trail at **1.6** miles. (To bypass the head, continue south on the main trail.)

Midway along the land link to Reservation Head is a Coast and Geodetic Survey elevation marker showing 6.32 feet above sea level. At high tide the head end of the strip gets pretty soggy, but a few ballet leaps will get you across. On firmer ground, ignore a rough trail up to the right, but take the left choice. The trail soon splits. Go left. Reservation Head is crowned with three very different jewels of its own, and the first stop is Lottie Point, **2.0** miles from parking.

The point, a half city block in size, and a 20-foot-high mass of rock with enough soil to sponsor a few trees and shrubs, is on the Deception Pass side of a narrow, rock-walled channel. Cross the channel on gravel at low water; at other times crossing the moat might require dashing between opposing surges of waves.

On the outer edge of the point look left, pretty much east, across the mouth of Lottie Bay and into the canyon of Canoe Pass. Both spans of the bridge are in full view, as is the 10-knot current of Deception Pass.

Back on the loop trail, another short jaunt leftward finds you looking down a fearsome chute of clay, gravel, and roots to a channel larger than at Lottie Point. The view is of a larger subheadland named Lighthouse Point, **2.2** miles from the trailhead. Getting out there is tough and dangerous, so just look and admire.

Leaving Lighthouse Point behind, the trail swings more to the north and onto higher ground. At **2.3** miles, a side trail doubles back sharply left (northwest) and climbs to more of everything on Reservation Head proper: more view ledges, more moss-bedecked bedrock corridors, and more of the bonsai-like pines and firs of the wind-shear coastal zone.

This diversion, a quarter mile out and back, is not a loop. Out on the northernmost reaches of Reservation Head, look down on Bowman Bay and back to Rosario. On the loop trail once more, a final 0.4 mile leads to closure and to rejoining the main trail, **3.0** miles in all.

Walking south, now on the Canoe Pass Trail, the path stays near the water briefly, with several unsigned paths to its left. Ignore them. Upon reaching vertical cliffs plunging into the bay, the track switchbacks upward among

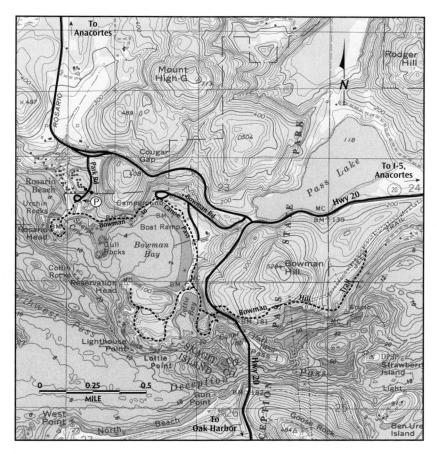

tortured treescapes clinging to a veneer of soil. Just shy of a half mile from the link to Reservation Head, and after the path has flattened out and the water appears to the south, find a well-used trail to the right, and go down it. On a grassy shelf 30 feet above the green water, **3.4** miles from the trailhead, you will be looking right into the maw of Canoe Pass.

For the return, continue northward along the main trail until it drops to a saddle and a four-way junction. Go left for a pleasant 0.2-mile return to the Canoe Pass Trail. At that point turn right and back the way you came. Skipping the headlands, it is 1.8 miles from the view stance on Canoe Pass to the parking area at Rosario Beach.

33 Goose Rock

Distance: 3.5 miles round-trip
Time: 3 hours
Starting elevation: 180 feet
High point: 484 feet (Low point: 10 feet)
Trail type: Forest trail to open ledges on summit
Avalanche potential: None
Difficulty level: Moderate to strenuous
Map: USGS Deception Pass (7.5' series)

The Hike

Goose Rock is essentially an oval with both the Perimeter Trail and a summit route, the Goose Rock Trail. There is much beauty along both, so merely choosing one over the other leaves out too much. With the many connector trails available, a kind of lumpy figure eight is possible, and you can see it all.

See page 99 for a map showing this hike.

Lighthouse Point on Reservation Head, from West Summit of Goose Rock.

Getting There

See the introduction to Deception Pass State Park (pages 95–96) for general directions to the area.

On the Whidbey Island end of the bridge, find the bridge-view parking area at milepost 41.7, and park there. Directly across State Route 20 is the Goose Rock trailhead.

The Trail

Shortly into the woods ignore a trail to the left, but take note of two more off-shoot trails before arriving at the summit ridge. These, together with the stretch of Goose Rock Trail between them, constitute a part of the figure-eight design. For now, go up **0.3** mile to the open ledges.

Goose Rock is a ridge with two distinct summits. As you arrive, Southeast Summit is to the left, and higher Northwest Summit is up to the right. Like everyone else, though, first rush forward for an eyeful of view over a lot of country. Then hurry up to the right and the true summit at 484 feet.

Most of the open view is south and west, but by moving around a bit you can tease out some major sights north and even east. West, look out over the park's North Beach to West Point, or to Deception Island a bit north of due west (288 degrees), which sort of guards the west entrance to Deception and Canoe Passes. Cranberry Lake is southwest at 230 degrees, and over the barrier strip of trees behind it are the sand dunes of West Beach. Also visible are the San Juan Islands, the Olympic Mountains, Vancouver Island, and, of course, Mount Rainier.

Head abuzz? Shake it off and sprint to Southeast Summit for a super slice of the central Cascades. There is the icy cone of Whitechuck Mountain, standing to the left of huge Glacier Peak, then Mounts Whitehorse, Bullon, Three Fingers, and Liberty, all four on the same long rock bastion.

Look down at the bedrock, too. Read the cast-in-stone story of the glacier's passage, the northeast-to-southwest gouges in the rock.

Find the beginning of the down route directly between the twin sets of power lines that plunge off Southeast Summit. Do not skip down this section of trail, though. It is nicely laid out but is steep and twisted and requires some care. A half mile below the top, **0.8** mile from the trailhead, join the Perimeter Trail on Cornet Bay. Go left (east) along the water, soon climbing from the 10-foot level to 140 feet to go over a bluff.

Descending the rocky head, you get a spectacular view of Mount Baker. The tops of North and South Twin Sisters are in the picture as well, etched against the backdrop of Mount Baker and its seasonally white Black Buttes. The trail turns more northeasterly at the bottom of the descent from the cliffs, **1.1** miles along.

Close to the water now, the way passes Ben Ure Island out to the right. The pleasant route is up and down for a time in deep forest solitude. When it crosses beneath the second of two sets of power lines coming across from Bowman Hill, look left (south) for a side trail.

Here, the **2.1**-mile mark, leave the Perimeter Trail to begin recrossing the oval. Climb moderately upward to the Goose Rock Trail in 0.3 mile. Go right on Goose Rock Trail, back the way you came earlier. In a scant 0.1 mile, go left (southwest) and down to rejoin the Perimeter Trail. The junction is an open, ledgy place that invites notice. A quarter mile down the hill, at **2.4** total miles, go left at another junction to reach Cornet Bay at the **2.7**-mile mark of the trip. Take a right on the Perimeter Trail to a pedestrian tunnel beneath SR 20 in 0.4 mile, **3.0** miles so far.

A short distance west of the tunnel is a gate. Go right and downhill on a dirt connector road, then continue on paved park road. In a quarter mile, the road ends at parking for North Beach, just above the swift waters of Deception Pass. Pick up the continuation of the Perimeter Trail at the right (east) end of the parking area.

The quarter-mile walk up to the bridge-view parking area is studded with scenery and huge old-growth Douglas firs. Just before reaching the bridge, look out over the turbulent waters to Lighthouse Point and tiny but deep-set Lottie Bay on the Fidalgo shore. When you absolutely must, climb the steps to the parking area, 3.5 miles in all.

34 Bowman Hill Trail

Distance:	2.0 miles round-trip
Time:	2 hours
Starting elevation:	180 feet
High point:	380 feet
Trail type:	Forest and cliff rim
Avalanche potential:	None
Difficulty level:	Easy to moderate, some strenuous
Map:	USGS Deception Pass (7.5' series)

The Hike

Among the many wonders of Deception Pass State Park, Bowman Hill Trail may be one of its best-kept secrets. Intentional or not, there are no signs of any kind marking this approach to the best high views of Pass Island, the bridge, and Canoe Pass from its east end. Views across Deception Pass to Goose Rock and down to Strawberry and Ben Ure Islands are good as well as precipitous.

See page 103 for a map showing this hike.

View from the clifftop trail on Bowman Hill.

Getting There

See the Deception Pass State Park introduction (pages 95–96) for general directions to the area.

At milepost 42.2 of State Route 20, at the Fidalgo Island or north end of the Deception Pass Bridge, two small crescent-shaped parking turnouts allow for bridge viewing. Park at the one farthest away from the bridge (0.1 mile) and look directly east across SR 20 to where the rocky cliffs grade off to dirt embankment and forest. About 20 feet north of the last vertical rock is the start of the Bowman Hill Trail.

The Trail

For **0.3** mile the trail rises along with the cliff. It parallels the highway as the latter heads for the bridge. At 275 feet in elevation, a ledge provides a great view down upon the bridge approach and into the turbulent waters of Canoe Pass. An abrupt turn leads off into sparse woodland studded with madrona trees. The trail passes over beautiful, moss-draped bedrock basalts.

Gently rising terrain draws the trail to a startling return to the brink in **0.5** mile. Dizzying cliffs drop away 380 feet to the swirling waters of Deception Channel. The gulf looks more like the aftermath of a cataclysmic slide, and not too long ago, either. Be very attentive to your footwork along the rim.

The smaller island below and left is Strawberry. The inhabited one, beyond which is the marina on Cornet Bay, is Ben Ure. Out over Strawberry Island is Hoypus Hill. The power lines nearly overhead arc all the way to Goose Rock in the Whidbey Island half of the park.

Leaving the lofty view, climb a little more and pass beneath the second set of three-strand power lines, where the trail presents three choices. Leftward and up, climb to the topmost of the power poles at 440 feet, with views south to Ault Field and Whidbey Naval Air Station and east over Mount Vernon and into the Cascades.

Turn right to the east edge of the bowl-shaped gash in Bowman's side and to more spectacular views of island magic. From this prow, you look directly into Canoe Pass as it slices along the shore of Pass Island.

The third choice continues along the main trail, which starts to drop steeply. For another 150 vertical feet down, many private viewing and picnicking opportunities abound, then only forest. Call it **1.0** mile and far enough at the last of the vista ledges, but the trail, mostly as power line right-of-way, goes all the way into the community of Dewey.

35 Hoypus Hill

Distance: 3.8 miles round-trip
Time: 2.5 hours
Starting elevation: 30 feet
High point: 260 feet
Trail type: Old-growth forest trails
Avalanche potential: None
Difficulty level: Easy to moderate
Map: USGS Anacortes South (7.5' series)

One down, hundreds standing: the old-growth wonderland on Hoypus Hill.

The Hike

On this hike you don't climb anything monumental, and its distant views fall a bit short of rave, yet Hoypus Hill is in a class by itself. It is a broad peninsula jutting out into Deception Pass Channel toward Similk Bay, and it is a sprawling repository of old-growth forest, sighing with timelessness. If you have to suppress silly grins and tree-hugging urges when among the big ones, Hoypus will test your mettle.

Getting There

See the Deception Pass State Park introduction (pages 95–96) for directions to the area.

At milepost 40.8 of State Route 20, turn east on Cornet Bay Road. At 1.3 miles, pass the boat launch site and reenter Deception Pass State Park, signed for Hoypus Point Natural Forest Area. At 2.1 miles park at an unused gravel pit. The trail, a gated road, angles off to the right.

The Trail

Most of the trail is flat to gently rising, allowing you to spend your time and effort treetop gazing. The forest is heavy with 450-year-old Douglas firs. There are lots of nice hemlocks, too.

At a scant **0.2** mile, note a trail coming in from the west: This is the reentry trail that completes the Hoypus loop. Ignore or explore another right turn at **0.4** mile, but keep on truckin' northeast, slowly leaving Cornet Bay.

Periodically, large and healthy Sitka spruces appear, and these are a special delight for their rarity in the Lower 48. The bark of these trees is composed of rounded scales that look like coins overlapping one another, and their trunks frequently bell out before entering the earth. At about **1.0** mile, some nice western red cedars can be found, and lots of great old firs, too. For its strain on neck muscles, think of this stretch as the "Ben-Gay Mile."

At **1.1** miles from parking, the trail heads due south and along the wooded side of private dwellings. Past the houses, the trail runs up against the park's southern boundary where there is a 20-foot-long link with a private forest road. Go right (west) with the trail, and start the only serious climbing of the route. It's steep, but for only a quarter mile. The hilltop (260 feet) marks **1.7** total miles.

If coming up was serious upping, there is some semiserious mudding to be done on the other side. At **2.3** miles, encounter a junction and turn right

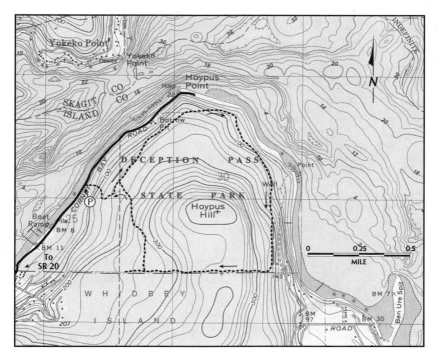

(north). In 0.4 mile more, ignore a left turn and curve northeast. At **3.3** total miles, seeing splashes of Cornet Bay through the trees, turn right at another junction, which leads back to closure of the loop and rejoins the entry trail in a quarter mile at the **3.6**-mile mark of the walk. Trailhead is down to the left just 0.2 mile farther.

Massage those neck muscles, then head for another Deception Pass delight.

36 Fort Ebey State Park

Distance:	3.8 miles round-trip
Time:	4 hours
Starting elevation:	30 feet
High point:	200 feet (Low point: 0 feet)
Trail type:	Forest, bluffs, and beach
Avalanche potential:	None
Difficulty level:	Easy to moderate
Map:	Whidbey Island, King of the Road Maps (available at bookstores and convenience stores, or call 1-800-223-8852) or USGS Port Townsend North (7.5' series)

Beach strolling at Fort Ebey State Park.

The Hike

Fort Ebey, built in 1942 to guard critical shipping lanes, was never needed. In 1980, it became the wonderful park it is today. It has lots of trails, bluffs, views, and interesting geology to explore.

Getting There

From the south, take Interstate 5 Exit 189 to Mukilteo, and ferry across to Clinton. Drive State Route 525 north to join SR 20. At milepost 26.6, turn left onto Libby Road, signed well in advance for Fort Ebey State Park. On Libby Road, follow the signs to the park registration booth in 1.8 miles. At the booth the road splits. The right turn leads down to a very small beach parking area.

From the north, take I-5 Exit 230 in Burlington, and follow SR 20 west and then south all the way to Libby Road at MP 26.6. Then follow the directions above.

The Trail

From the parking area, walk north a tenth of a mile on road. A few feet east of the rest rooms, pick up the trail to tiny Lake Pondilla. The lake is interesting because of its origin, not for its inherent beauty, for it lies in one of many pits scattered throughout the park. This type of topography is called hill and kettle. It can result when retreating glaciers leave behind huge blocks of ice. Outwash fills around the stranded bergs with soils and gravels, and when the ice melts away, deep pits or "kettles" surrounded by ridges or "hills" remain.

From the lake, continue west via trail down to the beach with its small, log-filled lagoon. Spot Mount Constitution on Orcas Island just shy of due north. Port Townsend is due south. Walk the short beach to its south end, then, just past the choking lagoon, follow a trail back up to the beach parking area, **0.6** mile so far.

The Bluff Trail heads south from parking. On the way, it passes the modern light on Partridge Point. (You don't want to be there when the horn sounds.)

View opportunities abound from the bluff, but watch out for breakaway endings on the many side trails to the brink. The sea is winning back coastline here. After 1.0 mile of bluff, the path arrives at a picnic area and the remains of some big gun emplacements and bunkers. Go in and out at will.

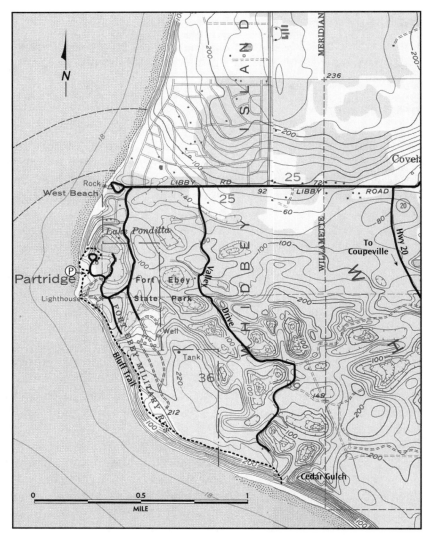

The bluff is a wide treeless area here. Explore it all, even down to the water, then continue south on the trail. When you reach the deep, brush-filled ravine of Cedar Gulch, the **2.2**-mile point, it might be time to go back. In a place named "Cedar Gulch," things could get a little rough.

It is 1.6 miles from gulch to parking, **3.8** miles in all.

37

Ebey's Landing

Distance:	3.6 miles round-trip
Time:	3 to 5 hours
Starting elevation:	0 feet
High point:	240 feet
Trail type:	Beach and bluff walk
Avalanche potential:	Snow, none; earth, slight
Difficulty level:	Easy; bluff climb, strenuous
Map:	Whidbey Island, King of the Road Maps (available at bookstores and convenience stores) or USGS Coupeville (7.5' series)

The bluff and beach at Ebey's Landing, seen from the trailhead.

The Hike

A trip to Ebey's Landing will set your mind to buzzing by day's end. It combines an always special beach walk with a return along a 240-foot-high bluff that looks out over the waves. The whole area is so rich in Washington history that in 1978, along with Fort Ebey State Park and much of the Coupeville area, it was named the nation's first National Historical Reserve.

Getting There

From the south, drive Interstate 5 to Exit 189 and go west to Mukilteo, then ferry across to Clinton. From there, drive State Route 525 north to its intersection with SR 20. Continue north on SR 20 to milepost 22.2, which is 0.3 mile north of the Coupeville pedestrian overpass. Turn left (west) on Ebey's Landing Road for 1.6 miles to Ebey's Landing, with parking, beach, and trailhead all in one place.

From the north, take I-5 Exit 230 in Burlington, and drive SR 20 all the way to Coupeville. The turn onto Ebey's Landing Road will be a right (west) at MP 22.2, with the pedestrian overpass in sight.

The Trail

It doesn't matter which way you do the loop, but consider the tide. Waves squeeze the bluff at high tide along part of the beach portion of the hike. With a bit of high stepping and maybe a sock full of water, you can get through most any time. There is no danger of entrapment by high water.

Walk northward on the beach or on the trail from the parking area. In a half mile the rising bluff bulges toward the water, and you will either be shuffling across the sand or sidehilling the wave-washed stones at the high tide line. Well before the first mile, the beach widens greatly, making room for Perego's Lagoon, itself more than three-quarters of a mile long. One may walk the beach here, or along the lagoon, or both.

Though Perego's water has the look of an overpopulated zoo pond, we felt compelled to taste it to see if it was fresh or salt. The stuff seemed to be half and half, actually, and the mysterious body of water has no visible inlet or outlet.

At Perego's north end, the **1.7**-mile mark, a trail climbs steeply up the bluff in less than a quarter mile. At the top, turn right (south) and enjoy the sea wind in your face.

Be on constant eagle alert. They plane the thermals below you, hardly moving a feather the whole time. On the water, big ships and towing barges are

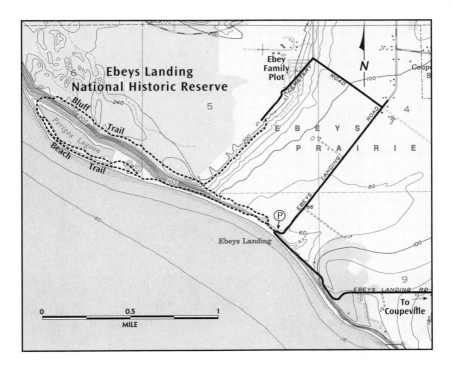

common sights, and pleasure craft paint frothy commas on the bright canvas.

Even in January you're likely to find flowers in bloom. Yarrow may be present along with gorse in golden flower. Look south to Fort Casey, and see Keystone–to–Port Townsend ferries dart out from behind the point. On a clear day, you will see all the way to Vancouver Island.

With the high point of the bluff behind, and an end to its margin of wind-sheared forest, the trail looks east and northeast over Ebey's Prairie. This land has been in continuous cultivation since Isaac Ebey claimed it in 1850. In his short life, he held many titles, but as customs agent he rowed the 10 miles back and forth to Port Townsend. In 1857, he was murdered by Haida Indians raiding from 400 miles north. They had no quarrel with Ebey, but a chief of their tribe had been murdered by whites in Canada, and Ebey was the only white "chief" they knew on whom to take revenge.

Partway down the bluff, **3.1** miles into the loop, a 2.0-mile round-trip trail leads to Sunnyside Cemetery where the true pioneer is buried. From this junction, it is a half mile downhill to complete the loop.

38 Boulder River Trail

Distance: 2.5 miles round-trip
Time: 2 hours
Starting elevation: 1,000 feet
High point: 1,180 feet
Trail type: Forest trail
Avalanche potential: None
Difficulty level: Easy
Maps: Green Trails Oso No. 77 and Green Trails Granite Falls No. 109

Picture Show Falls, tumbling into the rapids of Boulder River.

The Hike

Feature Show Falls along Boulder River Trail is a mesmerizing beauty of shimmering lace. More than that, the river itself is a thrashing marvel of white, green, and gray waters, and its valley is a designated wilderness of saved old-growth trees.

Getting There

Drive Interstate 5 to Arlington Exit 208, State Route 530, and drive east toward Darrington. A tad past milepost 41, turn right (south) on unsigned French Creek Road. In quick order, pass beneath power lines, then one or two driveways. Ignore all side roads and reach the trailhead in 3.7 miles. This popular trail has a small parking area, so it's best to turn your vehicle to face out.

The Trail

For quite a stretch, the way in is all flat on old logging road. At **0.3** mile, with the way so far trending southwest, round a gentle curve more to the south and hear for the first time the throaty voice of the Boulder River. This is the point at which the river valley's walls steepen to become more of a canyon.

When the road crosses a ravine spanned with old-growth logs and filled with rock and earth, you begin to sense what saved this river valley in its unspoiled condition. Also, in the railroad logging heyday of the early twentieth century, Boulder River Valley was deemed too small a pocket of timber with access making it too costly to log, so it was bypassed.

The river gets louder. At **0.6** mile it is more of a roar flung up from below. When you see several eroding impromptu trails slipping over the brink to the right, look carefully down through the trees. It is Boulder Falls you hear, and while it is possible to get down there, it is not easy, and there is no good place from which to see the action. The real tussle is coming back up.

Shortly beyond the falls comes Granny Grunt Hill. Granny is a departure from the spoil-you-rotten nature of the walk so far. The 170 feet of elevation gain take place in one slim tenth of a mile. Gird for it and go! Apparently the old road ended atop the hill. Real trail takes over from there.

After Granny, the trail parallels the river more closely, then drops to 30 or 40 feet above it. A little over a mile into the hike, the first of the unnamed falls hisses down the cliff across the river. It's pretty, but only a preview of coming attractions, with two or three more like it in the next half mile.

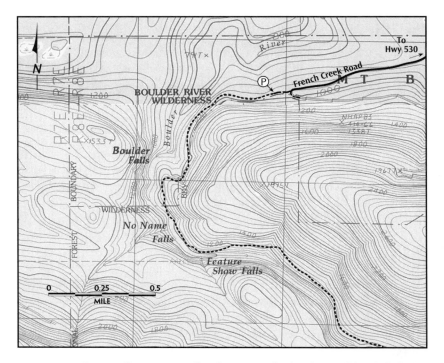

Feature Show Falls, at **1.25** miles, leaves no doubt about which falls is the real one. The cold, clear waters off Mount Ditney's northern flank gush over a cliff 110 feet above. A rib of rock then cleaves the jet in two, and this pair in turn divides and subdivides while dashing down the cliff face. By the time all of the trails, large and small, capillaries and arteries, reach the river, the veil is half as wide as it is tall. Endless variations play on this theme.

A few hikers look and hurry on, some snap a photo or two and go on, or go back. There are also those whose thoughts become tie-dyed with the falls' beauty. The eye is caught in the flow, then follows the spreading trail downward as it skips gaily from crevice to ledge. When river level is reached, it's back to the top to try again. Such is the pure fascination of motion blended with sound. The water comes down over the rock in a blend of sibilant stage whispers, then makes its sizzling exit into the dashing rapids of the Boulder River.

39 | Squire Creek Pass

Distance:	6.8 miles round-trip
Time:	6.5 hours
Starting elevation:	1,640 feet
High point:	4,000 feet
Trail type:	Forest roads and trail
Avalanche potential:	Moderate, caution advised
Difficulty level:	Moderate to strenuous
Map:	Green Trails Silverton No. 110

The Hike

Whitehorse Mountain from downtown Darrington and Three Fingers Mountain from just about anywhere are stirring sights. What they stir up in hikers is the need to be closer, to see them even better, and that's where Squire Creek Pass Trail comes in.

Getting There

Drive Interstate 5 to Exit 208, Sylvana–Arlington, and go east on State Route 530. At milepost 48.8, by the "Welcome to Darrington" sign, turn right (south) on Fullerton Street and drive four blocks to the intersection with Darrington Avenue, where a sign points right (west) to Squire Creek Road, the continuation of Darrington Avenue. Reset your odometer and turn right (west).

It is 5.8 miles from the end of Fullerton Street to the trailhead, if you can drive that far. The road, like the trail, is rough, and a badly eroded section at 5.3 miles may require you to walk the last half mile. There may be passenger cars up in there, so take your pick.

The Trail

Rock hop across the creek that ended the driving road and walk gradually upward. The roar of Squire Creek is a traveling companion, soon joined by sounds of rivers of water streaming down from the col between Mount Bullon and Whitehorse on the west wall of the valley.

At **1.0** mile, climb an old moraine and go down the other side to an easy crossing of a creek. The route begins to gain elevation at an increasing rate.

At times the route is one part trail and two parts creek, with a little mud thrown in. Watch your footing, for this trail has more rocks per mile than any other that comes to mind. Look up often enough, though, to gape at the many sentinels of the centuries, the big cedars and Douglas firs.

Above 3,200 feet, most of the switchbacks and the roughest portions of trail are past, and at **1.9** miles the route enters an open area beneath slab

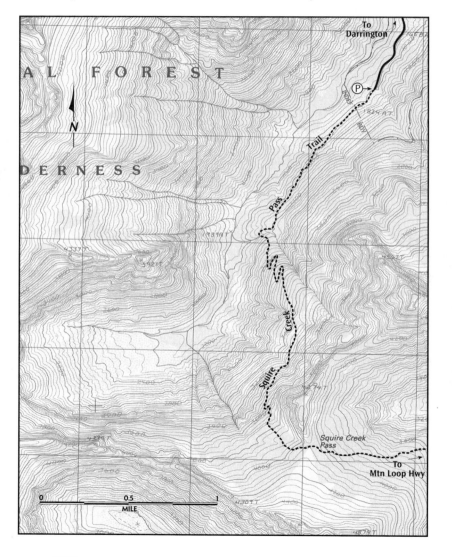

cliffs. In the next third of a mile the trail crosses three separate talus slopes. Caution is called for: With the proper snow and cornice conditions, possibilities for avalanching exist here.

West across the valley are 3,000-foot rock walls pouring meltwater into Squire Creek. Slightly southwest, and competing nicely for attention, are the 4,000 near-vertical feet of cirque headwall on Three Fingers Mountain. It's okay to stop and stare.

To the left of the trail at about **2.4** miles, rock walls above start curving east to form the north side of Squire Creek Pass, about a mile distant.

Walk the last third of a mile on ledge exposed by shimmering rivulets. Continuous bedrock is covered, if at all, by a thin veneer of precious soil, but the floor of the pass is bedrock flat and bare enough to host a hoedown.

Now you've got gazing rights east out over the Sauk River Valley as well. And many folks, with time and energy to spare, wander easily up the south side of the pass for more.

40 Beaver Lake Trail

Distance:	5.5 miles round-trip
Time:	3 hours
Starting elevation:	950 feet
High point:	1,140 feet
Trail type:	Forest and riverbank trails
Avalanche potential:	None
Difficulty level:	Easy
Maps:	USGS Whitechuck Mountain (7.5' series) or Green Trails Sloan Peak No. 111

Alders line the banks of the Sauk River along the Beaver Lake Trail.

The Hike

Beaver Lake is best described as the open-water portion of a riverine marsh, rich in biodiversity. Back from its shore is the shockingly vertical southwest face of Whitechuck Mountain, its summit 6,000 feet above. The trail follows the fast-paced Sauk River as it hurries down out of Monte Cristo, and the accompanying forest is a scroll of scenes changing with distance from the river. It alternates from sunny, bankside alders to the deep solitude of moss-draped firs. Big trees, 4 and 5 feet in diameter, are commonplace, and then the champion: a western red cedar, giant enough to warrant a sign of its own.

Getting There

Drive State Route 530 east from Interstate 5 Arlington Exit 208. At milepost 49 on the east edge of Darrington, turn right (south) on the beginning of the Mountain Loop Highway. Drive to MP 6, at the west end of a bridge over the Sauk River. Cross the river, turn right, and park at the trailhead.

The Trail

The trail drops to parallel the river on old railway right-of-way. The power of the Sauk is evident everywhere in old channels and the hushed rush of the channel of the moment. At points along the way look for the rugged profiles of Mounts Pugh, Sloan, and Bedal, names prevalent in the gold-fever history of the area.

At **0.3** mile the trail leaves the river to pass beneath the mossy limbs of old forest. Water fills ditches on both sides, but the trail is not muddy. Welcome little bridges cross drainage cuts in the former rail bed. Beaver Lake awaits at **1.1** miles, and a portion of it, too, is crossed on an aging, but strong, plank-and-post bridge. The south end of the structure lands on a peninsula, and it is here that Whitechuck Mountain shows its narcissism, staring at its own reflection in the pond.

At **1.6** miles, the power of the water is amply demonstrated as the trail ends at a 10-foot drop to gravel and water. For 75 yards what was once river-bank, with trail, is now silt on its way to the Skagit delta. The best way to sur-mount the problem is to climb a hundred vertical feet of brush-holding, grass-grabbing embankment, then go down the other side via the same stuff. Or, plow through the knee-deep muck.

On real trail again, walk amid standing monuments to the railroad logging days, a colonnade of trestle supports, some with remnant crossbars growing

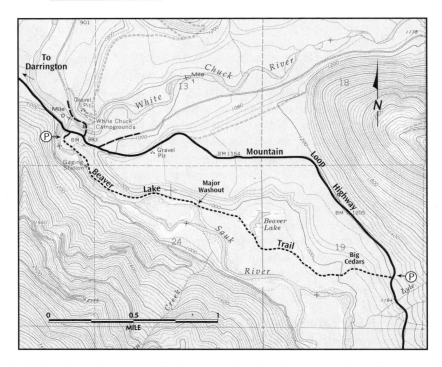

minigardens of mosses and shrubs. Look to the river where the trail used to be; a line of broken-off pilings in the water shows that the river has reclaimed more than the path.

Leave the river once more to walk a convoluted passage through quiet rain forest. Part of the trail is along a creek, which soon will join the river.

At **2.4** miles, in somewhat open woods, two massive cedars suddenly dominate the scene. Both are western reds, but the one on the north side of the trail puts a crimp in the brain and a crick in the neck. It is 15 feet in diameter, and that makes for 47 feet of circumference, plus.

The rest of the trail is not only anticlimactic but steeply uphill for a little over 0.3 mile. It ends at the southern Beaver Lake trailhead on the Mountain Loop Highway, **2.75** miles along. Walking back by road is about the same mileage as by trail, but not a fraction as interesting.

41 Green Mountain

Distance:	3.8 miles round-trip
Time:	2.5 hours
Starting elevation:	2,910 feet
High point:	3,805 feet
Trail type:	Blocked forest roads to summit
Avalanche potential:	Moderate, caution advised
Difficulty level:	Moderate
Map:	USGS Meadow Mount (7.5' series) or Green Trails Granite Falls No. 109

The Hike

Green Mountain is a treat because of its unique views of its better-known neighbors. It is directly across the South Fork Stillaguamish from Mount Pilchuck's rugged north slope, and closely southwest of the massive rock wall

Mounts Three Fingers and Big Bear from Green Mountain.

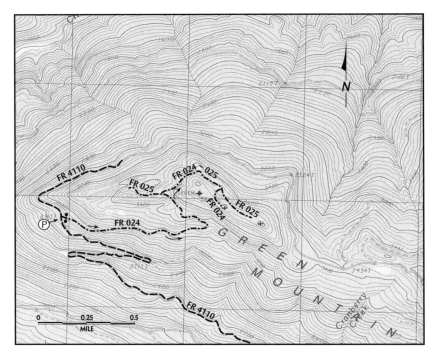

supporting a row of giants named Whitehorse, Three Fingers, Big Bear, and Liberty. Unique indeed.

Getting There

Drive State Route 92 east from its beginning on SR 9 just north of Lake Stevens. SR 92 ends at the east edge of Granite Falls, and the route becomes the Mountain Loop Highway. Go left (north) at the junction. At 15.5 total miles from SR 9, Green Mountain Road, also Forest Road 41, is found on the left.

Reset your odometer. In 1.9 miles the road splits three ways. (The right-hand option isn't much of a road.) The middle choice, FR 4110, is Green Mountain Road, and it goes as far as you can drive. Because of numerous side roads, the route description includes mileages and directions for side roads where a hiker could go wrong but ignores all other such roads.

At 1,900 feet (3.5 miles), FR 4110 curves hard left. Stay with it. (Straight ahead the road becomes FR 4111.)

At 5.0 miles, at a quarry, with two roads to the left (not likely to be taken seriously), FR 4110 swings hard right and up. If snow is a factor, the summit is very attainable from here and would add only 2.2 more miles round-trip to the hike.

At 6.1 miles (2,910 feet), park at a bermed, overgrown spur road on the right. A short distance in, a gun-blasted sign announces FR 024. This gated road is the route to walk.

The Trail

Most of the walk is moderately up while open views south and west keep coming. At **0.9** mile and 3,360 feet (no junction) the road switchbacks to the west and becomes noticeably steeper. Talus slopes of the summit ridge are visible ahead.

Though FR 024 goes to the summit, there is a broad intersection on the northwest crest of the main summit ridge at **1.2** miles (3,500 feet). Here, FR 025 comes in from the left (west) and runs concurrently with FR 024 for the next 0.4 mile. Go right, and up.

From the junction the road gets onto northern exposures. At 3,685 feet, and **1.6** miles from the trailhead, FR 025 continues straight while FR 024 turns hard right. Stay with FR 024. In a quarter of a mile, drag out a smile: the summit and road's end, 3,805 feet in the air.

Mount Pilchuck dominates the south view from 160 to 180 degrees. Big as it is, there are not many high places where you can get this close to Pilchuck. Eastward at 117 degrees is the megamass of Big Four Mountain. To the west, the valley opens wide as if to spill its greatness over a different kind of spectacular, the water world of Puget Sound. The angular skyline of Seattle is visible, too.

Then, the other reason for coming. Running from 52 to 96 degrees, northeast to east, is a continuous and truly gargantuan rock mass of 5,500- to 6,800-foot peaks. From the north, after Whitehorse, is Mount Bullon. It is nearly superimposed on Whitehorse at 54 degrees. Next, though not in the same range, is Jumbo Mountain, east of Whitehorse and across Squire Creek Valley and Trail (Hike 39). The most impressive, from this angle, is Three Fingers Mountain. It fills 3 or 4 degrees. Next is Big Bear Mountain, 84 degrees, or southeast, then the twisted spire of Liberty Mountain, at 96 degrees.

On the way down, for a better look at Liberty, go right on FR 025 to its end in 0.2 mile.

42 Monte Cristo Railroad

Distance:	3.6 miles round-trip
Time:	2.5 hours
Starting elevation:	1,000 feet
High point:	The end point is 840 feet
Trail type:	Forest, bottomland, and riverside trail
Avalanche potential:	Slight
Difficulty level:	Easy and moderate
Map:	Green Trails Granite Falls No. 109

The South Fork Stillaguamish River, rushing through Robe Canyon.

The Hike

Walk through Pacific Northwest history at its romantic best. This hike cannot match the antiquity of the cliff dwellings of the Southwest or the mystery of the lost civilization of Machu Picchu, but the ruins of the Monte Cristo Railroad do have the same echo of human struggle. Such is the legacy of crumbling rail bed and collapsing train tunnels in Robe Canyon near Granite Falls.

In 1889, when gold, lead, and silver were discovered in Monte Cristo, there were no foot trails in the area, let alone wagon roads. To get men and equipment in and the ore out, a railroad was planned up the rock-walled gorge of the South Fork Stillaguamish River. The struggle began, the rail line was eventually finished, but the river began to take it apart piece by piece long before the tracks reached Monte Cristo.

Getting There

Reset your odometer where State Route 92 begins, at SR 9 just north of Lake Stevens. Drive SR 92 east to its end on the east edge of Granite Falls. At that point, approximately 8 miles from SR 9, and right by the combined campuses of Granite Falls' middle and high schools, the route becomes the Mountain Loop Highway. Turn left and continue for a total of 15.5 miles. On the south side of the road a nicely styled, brick-framed sign announces the start of The Old Robe Trail. Park on the wide shoulder.

The Trail

A good gravel pathway pushes through a thick, dark canopy of trees to emerge on a bluff high over a marsh in about a tenth of a mile. Already the sound of the river is in the air.

A sign warns that, due to unstable conditions, the route is closed in 1.2 miles. Beyond the warning notice, the trail switchbacks down the bluff. At the bottom it skirts a marsh on old roadbed and approaches the river just upstream of Robe Canyon. When the trail splits at **0.9** mile, go left. (The two rejoin, but the right fork is often a quagmire.)

Two creeks require crossing, but they are not difficult to cross. Soon after the second creek, the river's decibel level rises and the gorge comes into view. You will begin to see timbers and then masonry work, which once supported an 80-ton steam locomotive along with its string of passenger and freight cars.

When you reach the **1.3**-mile mark, an impressive rock slide has wiped out a hundred-foot section of old railroad bed and pushed it into the river,

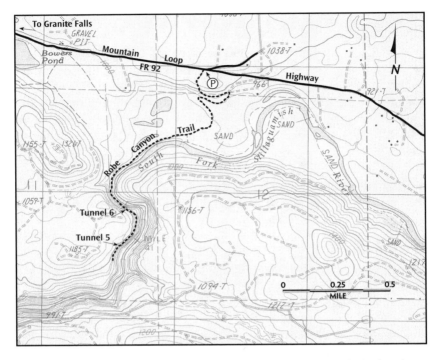

but it is not any more difficult or dangerous to cross than a typical talus slope. The river rages nearby, so, if you go this far, make your own decision regarding the surefootedness of your party and the conditions of the moment.

The **1.5**-mile mark brings in view both the rock slide and the maw of Tunnel 6. Tunnel 5, just 0.2 mile from the west end of Tunnel 6, is open as well. (Tunnel 7, up near Silverton and drilled through sand, was abandoned following repeated collapses.)

Pick your way over the boulders and tree debris of the slide, then go through Tunnel 6. One can see from end to end, so flashlights are not necessary. Tunnel 5 also looks to be very sturdy, but immediately outside its west end the riverbank is shorn away leaving a gulf that is unsafe to cross. A sign warns against going farther, so this is the **1.8**-mile point and end of the trail.

Natural events, like the big slide that doomed the Monte Cristo Railroad to failure, created this, and the Stillaguamish River is not yet finished with fine-tuning its gorge.

43 | Heather Lake Trail

Distance:	4.0 miles round-trip
Time:	3 hours
Starting elevation:	1,450 feet
High point:	2,590 feet
Trail type:	Moderately upward through mature forest
Avalanche potential:	Very little on trail
Difficulty level:	Moderate
Map:	USGS Verlot (7.5' series) or Green Trails Granite Falls No. 109

Heather Lake, in winter robes. The open water is at the lake's outlet.

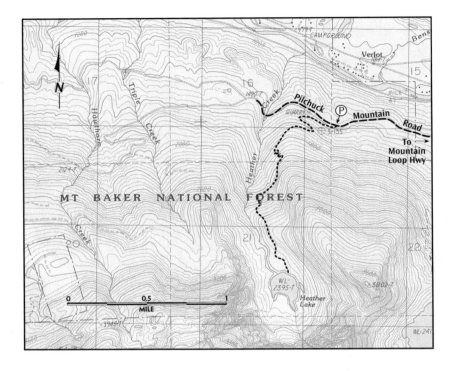

The Hike

Heather Lake is a gorgeous, glacier-carved mountain lake, and its trail is nicely planned and graded. It is usually walkable in all seasons, though from November to May it is apt to have snow on its upper sections and at the lake.

Getting There

Drive State Route 92 from its beginning on SR 9 just north of Lake Stevens. Follow through Granite Falls to the east edge of town where it ends. Reset your odometer at the left turn by the high school and middle school. The route is now called Mountain Loop Highway.

At 10.8 miles from Granite Falls, pass the Verlot Public Service Center. In another mile, right after the highway crosses the South Fork Stillaguamish River, turn right (south) onto Mount Pilchuck Road for 1.5 miles. At 12.3 miles from the city of Granite Falls is a large parking area for the Heather Lake trailhead. The trail starts on the east side of Mount Pilchuck Road.

The Trail

The lower reaches of this forest were logged in the 1940s and 1950s, and the guess is that minimal replanting was done. This particular second-growth forest is recovering spontaneously and is a nice place to be.

At **0.5** mile up, the trail intersects an ancient road and descends with it to the right. In less than 0.1 mile it comes to another intersection. Go left. A signless post sits in the crossroad to aid making the correct choice on the return. At **0.6** mile this road also fizzles, and real trail goes left and gets back to serious, though never more than moderate, climbing.

Now out of the former clear-cuts, old-growth trees begin to call out. A nice grove stands at the **1.2**-mile mark. After crossing a chute of slide alder, devil's club, and talus, many more of the imposing monarchs are seen. Go steadily upward on good trail in a beautiful wood. A half mile from the slide chute, the grade gentles at the high elevation for the day, 2,590 feet. From here it is less than a quarter mile, **2.0** miles in all, to the lake.

Heather Lake (2,450 feet) was cut out of the rock wall, a rib of Mount Pilchuck actually, which rises above its south shore. It was cut, chipped, twisted, and gouged one chunk at a time by eons of ice in successive waves. Can one stand and consider this drama and come away less than humble? The lake is pretty in any season, but especially so in soft winter whites. Snow draping rocks in the often unfrozen outlet area looks as if it is bending to drink the clear water.

44 | Lake Twentytwo

Distance:	5.0 miles round-trip
Time:	3.5 hours
Starting elevation:	1,000 feet
High point:	2,400 feet
Trail type:	Old-growth forest
Avalanche potential:	None on maintained trail
Difficulty level:	Moderate
Map:	Green Trails Granite Falls No. 109

Lake Twentytwo.

The Hike

Here is a biorich, protected, old-growth forest leading to a pretty little mountain lake at the foot of a spectacular 2,500-foot wall. Its trail is most often hikeable right through the snowy-season months, too. How can a nature junky go wrong?

The form of protection for this grand forest is somewhat unique. In 1947, the U.S. secretary of agriculture set aside 790 acres of virgin forest along Twentytwo Creek. The idea was to be able later to compare the plants, animals, and water quality of this undisturbed tract with the same in other parcels under "intensive management," i.e., timber harvesting.

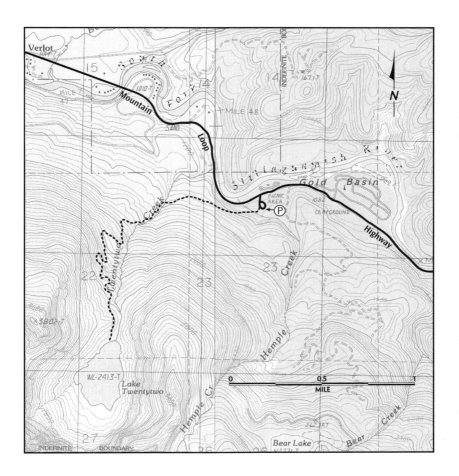

Getting There

Drive State Route 92 (from its beginning on SR 9 just north of Lake Stevens) to a T intersection on the east edge of Granite Falls where the state route ends. The route is the Mountain Loop Highway from here on. Reset your odometer. Turn hard left (north) with the highway there, soon passing the combined campuses of the middle and high schools. At 12.8 miles from Granite Falls, turn right (signed) to park at the trailhead.

The Trail

The path rises gently for a time. At **0.6** mile (1,340 feet), it crosses Twentytwo Creek over a good footbridge in the midst of a series of waterfalls. From this point on, sometimes near and sometimes a whisper in the distance, the plunging stream's course is followed to the lake. From the bridge on, the trail steepens moderately.

Again and again, progress upward is thwarted by gorgeous waterfalls. If the mesmerizing creek doesn't get you, the old-growth western red cedars surely will—and not just a few: There are a humbling great many of the giants.

At the 1,800-foot level **1.6** miles into the climb, the terrain changes. The trail emerges from the forest to angle up the west side of an old, alder-tangled talus slope. It does a couple of switchbacks before cutting across the top to reenter the trees. The trail is very rocky and rough from this point on.

There is another falls at the **1.9**-mile mark (2,260 feet), this one a tumbling slide of exceeding grace. In other seasons, a person could simply come to enjoy the first two miles of forest and falling waters—that is, not go to the lake—but with its mantle of frosted ice and background of snowy splendor in winter, the lake is a must.

Lake Twentytwo is a cirque lake or "tarn." Untold tons of ice, pressing downward from the rock wall on its south shore, gouged out a depression in the rock that later filled with rain and meltwater. Imagine forces powerful enough to scour bedrock to a depth of 53 feet, for there lies the bottom of Lake Twentytwo.

45

SNOHOMISH COUNTY

Big Four Ice Caves

Distance:	2.0 miles round-trip
Time:	1.5 hours
Starting elevation:	1,600 feet
High point:	1,860 feet
Trail type:	Beaver marsh and forest trail
Avalanche potential:	High near caves, extreme caution urged
Difficulty level:	Easy to moderate
Map:	Green Trails Silverton No. 110

The Hike

All winter, snow avalanches off the 4,000-foot north wall of Big Four Mountain, with much of it funneled to the base of a single, steep ravine. It comes with such frequency and volume that it cannot all melt, even in summer.

Wall of ice at Big Four Ice Caves.

139

Compaction and crystal deterioration turn the snow into ice, especially in the bottom layers. The result? A miniglacier in the making.

But there is more to the story. When melting or rain occurs, water plummets from the cliffs and into the same defile, and in so doing cuts a channel or "cave" beneath the ice.

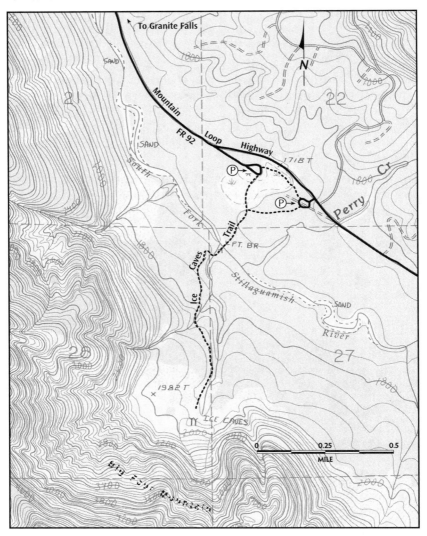

Big Four Ice Caves are wonderful to observe but dangerous indeed to go in or on. The plateau in front of the opening looks like it is repeatedly ravaged by floods, and the cave entrance is littered with collapsed sections of tunnel. Avalanches can come at any moment. Please heed the warning signs and stay out of the caves.

Getting There

Drive State Route 92 from its beginning off SR 9 just north of Lake Stevens. It ends at the east edge of Granite Falls, right by the joint campuses of the middle and high schools. Reset your odometer there and turn left (north) now on Mountain Loop Highway. (It has mileposts, but they tend to be a little sporadic.) At 25.3 miles from Granite Falls are a picnic area and the trailhead for the ice caves. If parking is tight, as it should not be in the snowy season, go back to the highway and drive another half mile east to a newer and much larger parking area. Both trail starts are well signed.

The Trail

Begin the route by crossing an active beaver marsh via a wooden causeway, then pass the link with the trail from the overflow parking area. (Wheelchairs can make the loop across the marsh and between the two entrances.)

Beyond the marsh, the trail crosses a creek and begins to climb, moderately at times. The forest is an aging one with all of the diversity of life forms that make such places pleasant. There are lots of mosses and lichen, and young hemlocks and cedars sprout from the nutrients of fallen giants.

At **0.9** mile the trail parallels the outwash from the caves, and the hiker enters the plain at the base of the wall of Big Four. Straight ahead is the yawning mouth of an ice tunnel, often two, changing form constantly, occasionally sealed off totally, even disappearing, though most often in place. Mounds of ice from collapsed sections lie as evidence out and away from the caves, and almost always the remains of fallen walls lead away from black openings, dwindling to nothing on the stones of the outwash. Hours of staring and wondering are possible here in the presence of natural events.

Big Four is a great destination when you don't feel like stirring too far from your conveyance, but it also couples nicely with the Lake Twentytwo Trail (Hike 44), or especially with the in-between distance down to the remnants of the Monte Cristo Railroad (Hike 42) in Robe Canyon.

46 SNOHOMISH COUNTY
Blue Mountain

Distance:	8.0 miles round-trip
Time:	5 hours
Starting elevation:	2,030 feet
High point:	3,064 feet
Trail type:	Forest road
Avalanche potential:	Slight
Difficulty level:	Strenuous
Maps:	USGS Lake Chaplain and USGS Wallace Lake (7.5' series)

The Hike

Blue Mountain, dorsal fin of a truly multiple-use wilderness playground, sits in the heart of expansive Sultan Basin north of the valley of the Skykomish. Its ridge runs some eight miles east and west. Although the principal reasons for entry to the basin concern timber harvest, drinking water, and hydroelectric power generation, view-addicted pedestrians know the real story: The roads are there to permit a wild bareback ride on Old Blue.

Getting There

Drive U.S. 2 east from Everett to Sultan. On the east edge of downtown, just barely past milepost 23, turn left (north) on Sultan Basin Road. It is well signed at possible points of confusion. After 12.8 miles on Sultan Basin Road you arrive at Olney Pass (2,030 feet) and a gravel road left (north) that goes to the summit ridge.

If you observe any snow on the road to Olney Pass, very likely you will have to walk from that point. If not, though steep and rough, the road does go to the high point, and most passenger cars can make it. There are plenty of turnarounds on the ascent.

The Trail

Almost immediately the gravel road splits. Take the left (west) fork. There are no other decision points in the **3.8** miles to the first summit at 2,955 feet. The

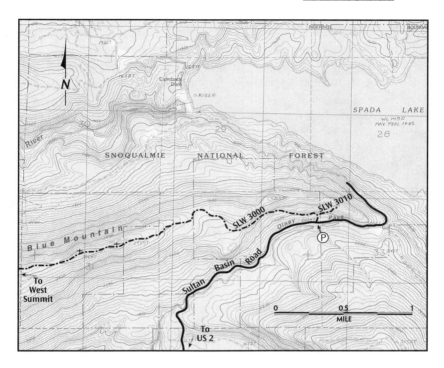

gate, referred to by a sign near the start, is located just beyond the second and highest summit at 3,064 feet.

Views prompt an intense rush the moment one breaks out into the open at the first summit. By all means, if you have gotten the car that far, leave it there and walk. The views are sudden and the ridge falls away on both sides as if pared with a knife. Blue Mountain is a ridge walk because there is no other place for the road.

From the second summit, a quarter mile away, a person can peer off the north side to the Sultan River 1,800 feet below. North across the Sultan spreads a rocky ridge with that maddeningly reoccurring name, Bald Mountain. No matter the handle, the place inspires wanna-go-there vibes.

Northeast, and peaking over the east end of Bald, is the fearsome-looking southwest wall of 6,135-foot Big Four Mountain, identifiable by its blocky form and telltale separated east peak (on a bearing of 65 degrees). More to the east, wave after spiky wave of high ridges and towers appear with names like Vesper, Del Campo, Sheep, and Sloan. Due east loom the broken and formidable steeples of the Monte Cristo Range. Southwest, discover even the man-made towers of downtown Seattle.

Trot back to the north side of the road and look northwest to a swath of homes and farms from Arlington to Silvana and Stanwood. Slices of Puget Sound spread beyond.

If you have the legs, there is more, west along the ridge. It's an easy round-trip walk of 1.5 miles to sights more to the northwest than can be seen from the high middle.

It is easy to spend three hours riding Old Blue.

47 | SNOHOMISH COUNTY
Wallace Falls

Distance:	5.0 or 6.6 miles round-trip
Time:	3.75 hours
Starting elevation:	320 feet
High point:	1,120 feet
Trail type:	Old road and forest trails
Avalanche potential:	None
Difficulty level:	Easy to moderate
Map:	Green Trails Index No. 142

The Hike

Above the famous falls, the Wallace River drains an area of some 20 square miles along the slopes of Mount Stickney, Prospect Peak, and Ragged Ridge. The squeezings are then funneled over the brink via Wallace Falls and on into the Skykomish River at Gold Bar.

Wallace Falls offers four viewing levels spread over some 900 vertical feet of trail. The planned 5.0-mile round-trip is based on going to the second of four established view sites, the Mid-level Viewpoint, which might have an edge in terms of its length of drop and sheer natural artform. The trail description beyond the Mid-level Viewpoint includes ministats for the Sky Valley and Upper Level Viewpoints.

Plan to go back again and again, for Wallace Falls's thunder is always fresh and always magnificent. Go early in the day, however, because this one has already been discovered.

Getting There

Drive U.S. 2 east from Everett to milepost 27.9 in Gold Bar. Turn left (north) at a Wallace Falls State Park sign. The 1.7-mile route is well signed from there.

The Trail

Leave the parking area on the power line right-of-way and plunge into second growth and richly diversified forest in **0.4** mile. Once in the woods the trail splits. Both go to the falls. The right-hand turn is the Woody Trail, the trail of choice. It drops to cross a small stream, then follows along the Wallace

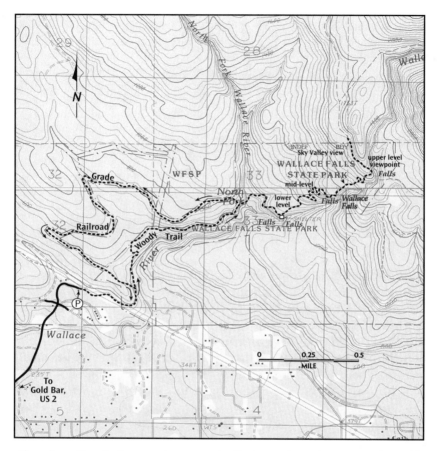

River for a time before veering away. It climbs moderately to a reunion with choice number two, the Railroad Grade, in **1.7** miles from parking. (The Railroad Grade takes an additional 1.25 miles to reach the same rejoining of routes but does it more gradually. Why not try them both?)

Shortly after rejoining, the trail crosses the North Fork Wallace River on a wide and sturdy footbridge. The North Fork drains a wholly different area from that of the parent stream, providing water for Shaw, Jay, and Wallace Lakes on the way. It joins the main fork in the forest not far below the bridge.

Though it seems like farther, just a half mile from the trail junction, or **2.2** miles from the trailhead (via the Woody Trail) a picnic shelter comes into view (elevation 870 feet). From the first of two positions at the picnic shelter, look upriver and see the leap of the big drop of Mid-level Falls through the trees.

Below you, its dashing outflow careens through a deep grotto. Then scoot down to another hold-onto fence to catch sight of the unbruised waters as they leap from the mountainside once more.

It gets even better than this 0.3 mile upward at the Mid-level Viewpoint, 1,120 feet in elevation. At **2.5** miles from the trailhead, it is also the planned turnaround point. A column of white water plunges 150 feet to a pool, then spills into a twisted flume to jet downward another 100 feet before dancing a frenzy to the grotto at the picnic shelter viewpoint. The stretch of trail leading here from the picnic shelter is often moderately strenuous, but is well worth a little extra effort.

Four tenths of a mile above Mid-level Falls, at **2.9** miles total and 1,400 feet in elevation, is the Sky Valley Viewpoint. It is actually two rail-fenced sites 30 yards apart. From there, though you are looking down on the falls' brink, the focus of the view is out over the Skykomish River Valley.

The last and Upper Level Viewpoint is another 0.4 mile above the Sky Valley site, but the trail becomes exceedingly rough. Though plain enough, it is like walking through a forest at the root-ball level. Upper Falls Viewpoint, **3.3** miles and 1,600 vertical feet from the trailhead via the Woody Trail, is like looking at Mid-level Falls in reverse order. The 50-foot plunge comes first, followed by the (at least) 150-footer.

Do resist going over the barricades—at any point—for that better look. Order your scenic drinks most any way you like, but please, not on the rocks.

48 | SNOHOMISH COUNTY
Three Waterfalls

Distance:	3.6 miles total
Time:	4.0 hours
Starting elevation:	720 feet for Sunset and Canyon Falls, 2,040 feet for Deception Falls
High point:	720 feet
Trail type:	Various: service road, abandoned rail bed, and maintained trail
Avalanche potential:	None
Difficulty level:	Easy, some moderate
Map:	USGS Index (7.5' series) for Sunset and Canyon Falls, USGS Scenic (7.5' series) for Deception Falls

The Hike

Two separate walks 20.0 miles apart along U.S. 2, the Stevens Pass Highway, comprise this outing. There is more here than the title suggests: The Deception Falls hike leads along the thrashing Tye River with its additional unnamed falling waters, and the day ends with a special treat of blackberry cobbler!

Fascination for living, dynamic water is right up there with staring for hours at the glowing coals of a waning campfire, but waterfalls go a step

The Tye River hits the wall—and is slowly cutting it down.

beyond the mysteries of fire. They shout out their power with earth-shaking force as if to proclaim that they must be heard.

Getting to Sunset and Canyon Falls

Take Interstate 5 Exit 194 at Everett and drive U.S. 2 to milepost 36.6, just east of the turnoff for Index. On the outside of a curve, pull into a large gravel turnout on the right (south). The only sign indicates that the road leading from the turnout is closed, but it is driveable downhill for 0.2 mile to parking at a bright red gate. Sunset and Canyon Falls are both approached from the single parking area.

The Trail

Walk around the gate and across a bridge spanning a man-made dry channel. Downhill a couple hundred feet the road splits. Left (east) goes to Canyon Falls, but for now, stay right and walk downward barely **0.3** mile to Sunset Falls. Rounding the next curve along the descent, see the start of the plunge while looking beneath the girders of a railroad trestle.

Near the bottom of the access road, cut left down a short, four-wheel-drive track to the blue steel rigging of fish-enhancement equipment 0.3 mile from parking. Use the good view ledge, or climb down over rocks to the runout below the falls. The entire South Fork Skykomish thunders between rock walls, dropping more than 90 vertical feet in less than a tenth of a mile: in a word, awesome.

Reel in the brain and convince it to steer your feet back uphill a quarter mile to the junction. Walk east (right), and reach Canyon Falls in 1.0 mile along old railroad grade. Total to here is **1.5** miles. Canyon Falls is similar to Sunset Falls, yet vastly different. The view of this cauldron is from a bridge back from its top or else along the north side of the drop.

Use extreme caution if you go out over the bedrock for a closer look. Portions of the way are downsloping and very slippery with algae. Even if you survived the first thirty seconds of a tumble into the churn, you know what waits a heartbeat downstream.

The river has carved the rock into many channels. At times all of them hold roaring jets of water, but when flow levels are highest the whole thing is a single, angry, white boil, flinging itself into the ravine below.

It is a mile back along the railroad grade, then right a short distance to the gate and parking.

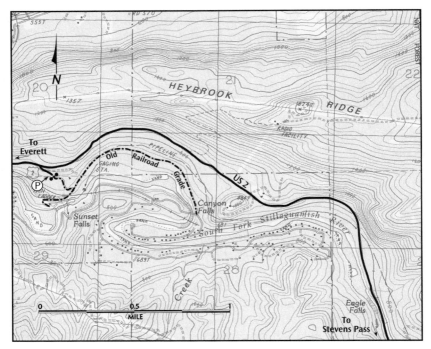

Getting to Deception Falls

Drive back up to U.S. 2, and proceed right (east) 20.0 miles to the Deception Falls parking area on the left (north) at milepost 56.8.

The falls are on Deception Creek and can be seen from the highway, but since few symphonies start off with crescendos, why would anyone do that to the viewing of a waterworks masterpiece? We shall see some other wonders first.

The Trail

Walk to the west end of the parking area and the paved start of the wheelchair-accessible portion of the route. In 150 feet, leave the pavement and go left on the trail and down some switchbacks through the hush of old-growth forest. The walkway is nicely signed with ecological information. In **0.4** mile, hear the call of the Tye River, and shortly come to the swift torrent about to enter a minigorge.

Leave the rapids and head upstream. Soon, take a stairway left and back down to the river. The full force of the water slams into a wall of seemingly immovable rock at right angles to the flow. A slot is being carved a molecule

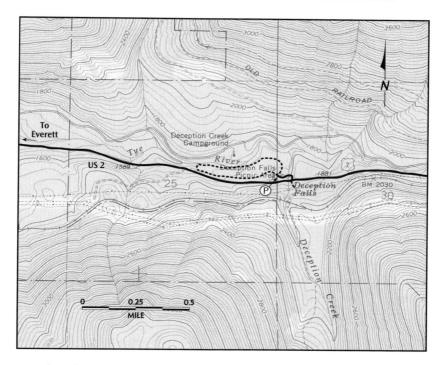

at a time in the barrier's center. Proceed up a gentle slope to a second stairway on the left, which leads to a powerful waterfall. Look upstream also, and see the joining of Deception Creek to the Tye River. They seem to be fifty-fifty in their contributions to volume.

Now head for the crescendo. Coming alongside Deception Creek, you cannot miss a pair of big western red cedars. At **0.8** mile, rejoin the paved way and go left, soon crossing the watery cauldron of Deception Creek. On the far side, walk a few feet upstream and pass beneath the highway on a catwalk barely 10 feet above the dashing frenzy. And the falls? How about six stars of deafening, spray-garnished emotion?

At last, we would say, you have earned the blackberry cobbler! Drive back west to the Index turnoff, MP 35.6, turn right (north), and in 1.0 mile cross the North Fork of the Skykomish River into town. Two blocks straight ahead is the Bush House, a hundred-year-old restaurant and country inn.

Of course, have the blackberry cobbler, and perhaps even a fine dinner for dessert.

49 | SNOHOMISH COUNTY
Index Town Wall

🥾🥾🥾🥾🥾

Distance:	2.4 miles round-trip
Time:	3 hours
Starting elevation:	1,720 feet
High point:	1,940 feet
Trail type:	Forest roads to cliff top
Avalanche potential:	None
Difficulty level:	Easy
Map:	USGS Index (7.5' series)

The Hike

The people of Index have a lot of things in common, and one of them is their backyard fence—more than a fence, really, for anything a thousand feet straight up certainly justifies the title of "wall."

Peaks of Skykomish Valley from Index Town Wall—the town is 1,200 feet below.

Daring types come to climb the thing, then rappel off in airy bounds. Others agree that views certainly must be fantastic from the top but are adamant about employing ordinary walking techniques to find out.

Getting There

Drive U.S. 2, the Stevens Pass Highway, east to milepost 30, 2.0 miles past Gold Bar. Turn left (north) onto Reiter Road. Reset your odometer.

In 0.8 mile, go straight as May Creek Road leaves left. Ignore a paved road right at the 2.4-mile mark. Ignore a rough-looking road to the left at 3.6 miles. At 3.9 miles from U.S. 2, turn left on a rough gravel road. (Reiter Road continues to the base of the wall and into Index, but you're being directed to the wall's top.)

At 5.1 miles the road nearly doubles back on itself from east to northwest. And shortly after, it passes beneath power lines, giving good views back down-valley. Ignore another turn, this one a right, near the power lines. A gate in the area is usually open. If not, parking and walking from the gate add only 2.4 total miles to an easy hike.

Park at a Y at 6.9 miles. The left, which goes on to Deer Creek Flat, is blocked to all except the power crowd. The Town Wall is out on the right fork, and although the road is driveable for 0.2 mile, there is no place at that point to park.

The Trail

Walk in **0.2** mile. What could have been a turnaround is a side road to the west, but the intersection is a huge mud hole. Go straight (south) and into more soup. Not to overstate the condition of this old road, but it could be mistaken for a kayak route. Do not be grossed away though, for the portages are easy and dry.

At **0.5** mile, progress is hindered by an "almost" bridge over Deer Creek. With care, a person can tease a passage over the rotting and rickety timbers. The creek is not dangerous, nor is the bridge high. Shortly after the crossing, the road forks. Go left. Mud holes reach the proportions of small beaver ponds, but again, they are easily avoided.

About halfway along, the road climbs just enough to leave the bogs behind. When road walking becomes a rather horizontal rock pile, **1.1** miles in, and the rocks veer sharply left (east), you are nearly to road's end at **1.2** miles.

And, oh wow, does it ever end! Fifteen feet farther on is the world's deepest and most sudden chuckhole. It is at least a thousand sheer feet to

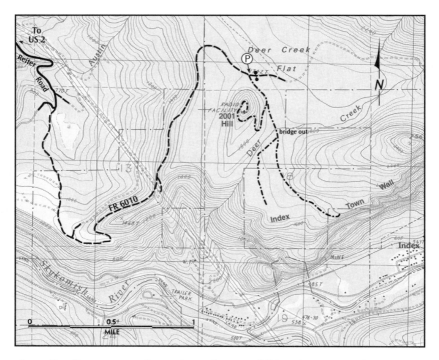

the valley floor. Footpaths push on for an additional quarter mile to more great view ledges, each one on the abyss, and each with its own unique perspective.

From the wall, you can see up the North Fork Skykomish only a short way, but the eye can follow the valley of the South Fork all the way to the backbone of the North Cascades. The big white peak southeast at 136 degrees is Mount Daniel, a few miles south of Stevens Pass.

The electrifying twin-towered titan in the wedge of land between the rivers east of Index is Baring Mountain. North from Baring are the amazingly serrated minarets of Mount Townsend, then Merchant and Gunn Peaks. Across Sky Valley are the splendid walls and towers of Mounts Index and Persis. Index is the one with a half mile of Bridal Veil Falls roaring off its flanks.

Whatever else can be said of this eyrie, it sure sits atop a backyard fence with an attitude.

50

SNOHOMISH COUNTY

Heybrook Ridge Lookout

Distance: 2.5 miles round-trip
Time: 1.5 hours
Starting elevation: 800 feet
High point: 1,720 feet
Trail type: Forest trail
Avalanche potential: None
Difficulty level: Moderate to strenuous
Map: Green Trails Index No. 142

The Hike

Heybrook Ridge is the last impediment to the joining of waters of the North and South Forks of the Skykomish River. They finally meet below Index, not far from the west end of the ridge. Despite being well under 2,000 feet in elevation, Heybrook seems to have an aura all its own. Perhaps it is only the shine from so many classy mountain neighbors.

Getting There

Take Interstate 5 Exit 194 at Everett and go east on U.S. 2 to milepost 37.6, 2.0 miles past the left turn to the town of Index. Park in a long, narrow, graveled parking area on the left (north) side of the highway.

The Trail

The trail starts at the west end of the parking area. A sign there implores hikers not to climb the lookout.

Unless there has been a miracle infusion of trail maintenance funds, expect rough going up the switchbacks until the track gains the ridge in **0.7** mile. For all of the water underfoot, there is very little mud.

The best views over to Mount Index and to Bridal Veil Falls on Index's north wall are found just below the summit. Unfortunately for viewing and photography, north slopes on the big mountain get little sun during most of the snowy season. It is mind blowing all the same, though, for Mounts Index, Persis, and Baring are all formidable structures with lots of vertical and lofty rock faces.

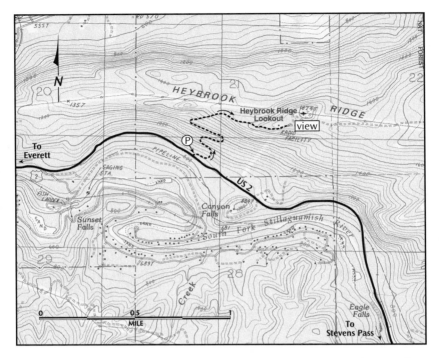

The main summit of Index is southwest at 227 degrees and more than 4,000 feet higher than Heybrook Ridge. In front of it is the "lesser" 5,500-foot middle peak, then the 5,400-foot North Wall. The latter is the most imposing of the three because it is right out front. East of Index is crag-laden Mount Persis.

The best place from which to ogle Baring Mountain and its tough-looking neighbors is from Index town proper, and, should one need additional incentives to go there, there is always the Bush House, the century-old country inn serving scrumptious desserts and dinners.

51 KING COUNTY
Maloney Ridge Lookout

Distance:	9.6 miles round-trip
Time:	6.5 hours
Starting elevation:	1,520 feet
High point:	3,364 feet
Trail type:	Forest roads
Avalanche potential:	Slight
Difficulty level:	Moderate
Map:	USGS Skykomish (7.5' series) or Green Trails Skykomish No. 175

The Hike

The best thing about lookout sites as view hikes is that they were originally chosen for that very reason, and Maloney Ridge is a standout in the crowd. The narrow ridge juts into the valley high above the town of Skykomish, making it a superb place from which to stand in awe of the great chasm that is the valley of the South Fork Skykomish River.

Mount Daniel, seen from the road up Maloney Ridge.

The name "Maloney Ridge" is really a misnomer, for the lookout site is actually on a rocky shoulder of Mount Sobieski. The real Maloney Ridge is off a mile and a half to the southwest. This is mentioned not to pick a fight but to prevent you from going off to find the wrong one.

Getting There

Drive U.S. 2 from Interstate 5 Exit 194 in Everett to milepost 50.6, a half mile past the Skykomish Ranger Station. Turn right (southeast) on a two-lane blacktop road signed simply for Forest Road 68 and also known as Foss River Road.

Reset your odometer and drive on. Cross the Foss in 0.8 mile. At 1.1 miles, ignore a side road left. Burlington Northern tracks are high overhead at the 2.4-mile mark. Stay on FR 68 heading south.

At 4.7 miles from U.S. 2, reach an intersection where FR 68 leaves left (southeast). The gated road straight ahead is FR 6840, and the way to go. Park here.

The Trail

Walk FR 6840 southward on flat ground. In **0.4** mile cross the Foss River in one of its more placid moods. Now the road nearly doubles back to head northwest and up. The **1.7**-mile mark brings a pleasant diversion as the road crosses a narrow waterfall. Once beneath the road via a tin tunnel, the water spreads, splashes, and glides steeply down the mountain on open, polished slabs.

At **3.5** miles (2,800 feet) lies an intersection where FR 6840 ends and the well-traveled road goes left. The route to the lookout continues straight ahead as FR 6848.

At 3,180 feet, look left and up the way of a playful, stairstepping waterfall. Seemingly, the gurgling stuff is coming from the base of the towers on the summit of Mount Sobieski.

A bit over a mile from the last road junction, **4.6** total miles from the gate, look for a highly visible spur road to the right on flat ground. Its sign is missing a numeral, but the road is FR 710. The nub of Maloney Ridge is a quarter mile out along the spur road.

Go by the communications building on its right side and follow a path. Where the lookout once stood is a rocky mound of pure delight poised on the edge of nearly vertical clear-cut forest. Then, let the feast begin: Lunch, of course, but the greater repast here is for the eyes.

The real reason for the quiet wonder of the scene requires a moment to comprehend. It is the immensity and the scope of the South Fork Skykomish

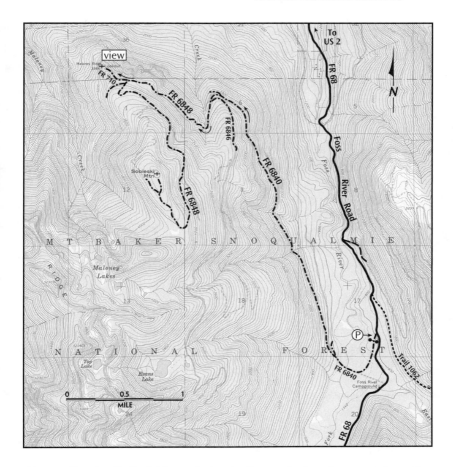

River Valley itself. Find Mount Index in the west, then turn and trace the valley east virtually to Stevens Pass.

By moving around a little, you can experience 300 degrees of sightseeing. The monster peaks grouped with Baring Mountain, northwest at 318 degrees, are all on a wedge of wilderness that separates the north and south forks of the Skykomish.

Going down the road, the eye can wander along the East Fork Foss River up its source on the huge snow dome of Mount Daniel, and just over the height of land to the south and up the West Fork lies the magic of the Alpine Lakes Wilderness.

So don't go down. Arrange for an air drop and go over the ridge.

52 Mount Zion

Distance:	3.6 miles round-trip
Time:	2.5 hours
Starting elevation:	2,950 feet
High point:	4,273 feet
Trail type:	Through forest to partially open summit
Avalanche potential:	None
Difficulty level:	Moderate
Maps:	Pargeter's Revised Pictorial Map of the Olympic Mountains or USGS Mount Zion (7.5' series)

The Hike

The summit fire lookout is gone, and the site is nicely cleaned up as well, but they could not take the views away with all of the crumbled timbers and steel. The growing young trees, however, are beginning to take care of that, so "do" Zion in the next few years.

Getting There

At milepost 292.7, 2.0 miles north of Quilcene on U.S. 101, turn west onto Lord's Lake Loop Road, and, after resetting your odometer, drive 3.4 miles to the base of an earthen dam. The impoundment is part of Port Townsend's water supply.

The road splits. Take the left fork, now Forest Road 28, and shortly enter Olympic National Forest. Gaining elevation, begin to see out over beautifully greened hills and junior mountains, enhanced by the absence of megacuts and the presence of many miles square of adolescent Douglas fir plantings.

At 4.0 miles from the dam, 7.4 total, encounter a three-way junction and bear right, still on FR 28. Reach Bon Jon Pass at 8.7 miles. At the pass, turn right (north) on FR 2810 for the final 2.0 miles to the trailhead, 10.7 miles from U.S. 101.

By inference, the presence of a modern pit toilet and large parking area at the trailhead means that Zion is a popular outing. For solitude, do it as a summit-view winter hike.

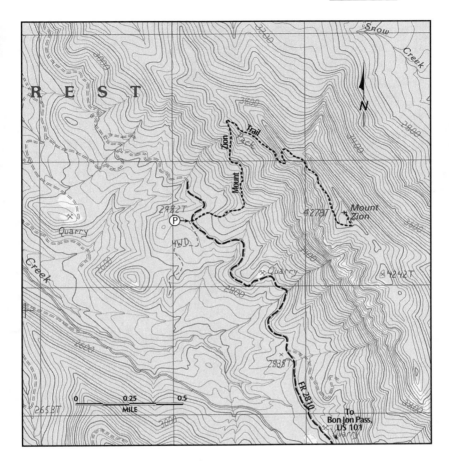

The Trail

No mysterious choices or junctions here. The trailhead is directly across from the parking area on the south side of the road, and the well-maintained, nicely graded trail rises only moderately through mature forest. There are even a few flat stretches; all in all, a painless, delightful walk.

Rhododendron predominates as understory shrubbery. Come back in April or May when it is in bloom. At 3,800 feet the switchbacks shorten and steepen as the rock mass of the summit nears. Thirty vertical feet below the mostly open, knobby top are some very nice campsites. For either camping or day hiking, do bring water. This is a dry trail all the way, and very likely so at any time of year.

Mount Townsend, 6,280 feet and off to the southwest, is the closest and most dominant feature in view, but the eye, with the aid of map and compass, can search for identifiable features for as long as the curiosity holds out. Mount Zion's stature as one of the highest front-runners of the Olympics, plus its position relatively near the Port Townsend corner of the peninsula, make it a grand pedestal for viewing far and wide.

53 Big Quilcene Lookout

Distance:	5.0 miles round-trip
Time:	4 hours
Starting elevation:	2,200 feet
High point:	3,450 feet
Trail type:	Forest roads
Avalanche potential:	Slight
Difficulty level:	Moderate
Maps:	USGS Mount Walker (7.5' series) or Quilcene District Olympic National Forest topo

Licorice ferns and sword ferns along the Big Quilcene River.

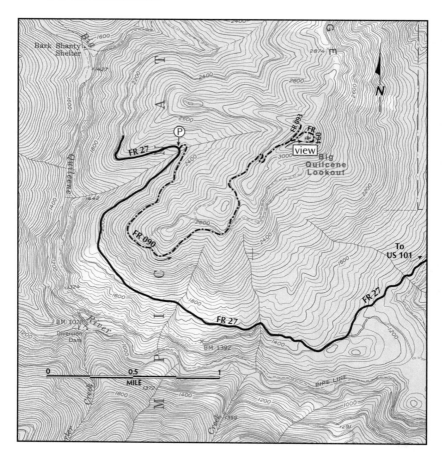

The Hike

Big Quilcene tops the south end of its range, a land mass that runs north and south for some 10 miles. In the north, the Little Quilcene River comes down out of Bon Jon Pass, bumps the range, and is nudged to the east. The Big Quilcene River comes out of the Buckhorn Wilderness and is forced to do a U-turn, legally it is assumed, around the south end of the ridge. Both empty into saltwater a half mile apart.

It's a sad refrain, but the lookout is gone. The lookout site gets a lot of attention from the noise-toys crowd, so do "the Big Q" as deep into the snowy season as weather conditions allow. Nothing shatters a reverie quite like an infernal combustion engine at maximum rpm.

Getting There

Drive U.S. 101 to milepost 296, 1.3 miles south of the town of Quilcene. A road on the west side of the highway at that point is signed Penny Creek Road but will soon be identified as Forest Road 27 as well. A good landmark for the turn is the Penny Creek Quarry, plainly visible as you approach the turn on U.S. 101 from the north.

In 1.4 miles, FR 27 leaves Penny Creek Road and goes off to the left. Stay left. At 7.0 miles from U.S. 101, park at a sometimes gated side road to the right (east) signed for FR 090.

The Trail

FR 090 goes to just below the west side of the summit. Take the right fork, now FR 094. It winds almost completely around the steepening ridge top to end at the lookout site 2.5 miles from FR 27.

In winter solitude, it's a 2.5-mile dreamwalk in lots of wide-open spaces all the way to the partially open top of Big Quilcene. On the way up, the over-the-shoulder backdrop view is the big front row of Olympic peaks: Constance, the Warrior Peaks, Buckhorn, and, closer still, Mount Townsend. From the top, more of the same, but all at a sitting.

To the northeast, if you can wiggle through the trees, nothing except weather hides a view of Mount Baker. Mount Walker screens the southeast yet serves as a reminder to go there (Hike 56). And to the south, horizons are limitless over the Big Quilcene River Valley, Tunnel Creek, and miles of canal country.

54 | JEFFERSON COUNTY
Mount Jupiter Ridge

Distance:	7.2 miles round-trip
Time:	4.5 hours
Starting elevation:	1,040 feet
High point:	2,000 feet
Trail type:	Clear-cut forest roads
Avalanche potential:	None
Difficulty level:	Moderate
Maps:	Quilcene District Olympic National Forest topo or USGS Mount Jupiter (7.5' series)

The Hike

Not far from the Brothers and Mount Constance, Mount Jupiter is on a ridge long enough to have its head out back with the big ones and its feet in the foothills. Flanked all the way to saltwater by two deep river valleys, the Dosewallips and the Duckabush, its eastern ridge has great relief, spelled v-i-e-w-s, from all angles.

Getting There

Drive U.S. 101 to milepost 309.5 at Black Point. Turn west on Mount Jupiter Road, signed "Mount Jupiter Trail 6 Miles." (Don't believe the 6 miles until you learn whether a key gate is locked or not. It is usually closed to vehicles from October 1 to May 1 for wildlife habitat protection.) The road is also Forest Road 2420.

At 0.8 mile stay left, actually more straight ahead, at a junction. Ignore side roads to the 1.7-mile mark where the route passes under power lines for the first of many times. At 2.4 total miles from U.S. 101, and nearly beneath the lines, find ample parking carved into the right-hand roadside. Most of the landscape here is entirely out in the open.

The gate is a tenth of a mile or so ahead. It is possible to drive up to have a look, but if it is locked, turnaround is tight and there is definitely no room to park.

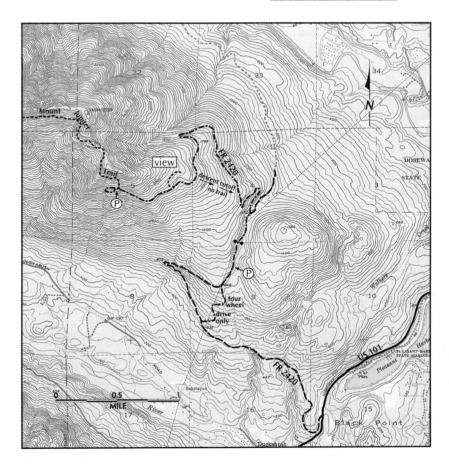

The Trail

Begin calculating the walking mileage from parking. In **0.4** mile ignore a road to the right and follow the curve left. Go under the power lines a last time and start to climb. It is nearly three miles to the next decision point, all in continuous clear-cut, so relax and plod on. Rise higher, and the expanding universe theory becomes more believable with each step, for views burgeon also.

At **3.3** miles is a very skinny and somewhat rough Y in the road on flat ground. Go right and climb steeply, but only for a final three tenths of a mile to a large log-loading platform on the right at the crest of the broad ridge. This is your window on the world, 2,000 feet above sea level, **3.6** pleasant miles from the gate.

Views east are limited only by visibility. In good weather, three volcanoes may be seen: Mount Baker northeast at 40 degrees, Glacier Peak at 71 degrees, and Mount Rainier southeast at 138 degrees. Mount Adams is behind Rainier. And St. Helens? It wasn't tall enough to be seen from Jupiter Ridge *before* it blew its cool.

55 Mount Townsend

Distance:	8.2 miles round-trip
Time:	6 hours
Starting elevation:	3,400 feet
High point:	6,280 feet
Trail type:	Forest trail to summit
Avalanche potential:	Extreme caution advised
Difficulty level:	Moderate to strenuous
Maps:	USGS Mount Townsend and USGS Mount Zion (7.5' series) or Custom Correct Buckhorn Wilderness topo

The Hike

So, what is a 6,000-footer doing in a collection of hikeable-in-the-snowy-season outings? The simple answer is that Mount Townsend sits smack in the middle of the Olympic rain shadow and receives relatively little precipitation compared with other peaks its height. However, when it comes to predicting snow levels, answers are rarely that simple. From mid-November through April, a hike on Mount Townsend may indeed be unrealistic. Always inquire about conditions in advance, and have a less ambitious alternative in mind.

Getting There

Drive U.S. 101 to milepost 296, 1.3 miles south of the town of Quilcene. Turn west on Penny Creek Road, soon identified also as Forest Road 27. In 1.4 miles, FR 27 leaves Penny Creek Road and goes off to the left. Stay left. At 14.6 miles, turn left (west) on FR 190, signed "Service Road." Drive to the upper trailhead at the road's end in just under a mile, 15.5 total miles from U.S. 101. The parking area is small for the trail volume, so arrive early or face additional walking in order to park elsewhere along the narrow service road.

The Trail

The trail starts switchbacking almost immediately, moderately upward at first, through mature forest. In **0.8** mile (4,100 feet), enter the Buckhorn Wilderness, and, if lucky, have a chat with the resident deer, a more curious

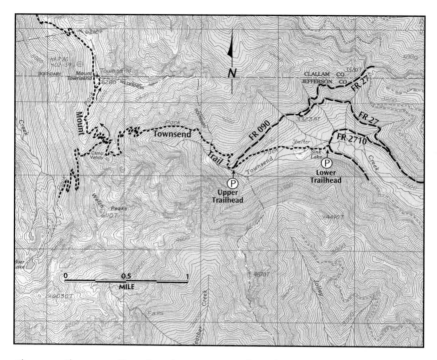

than cautious yearling doe that moves only a few feet off the trail before staring back.

At 4,500 feet the open slopes begin, and with them steepening trail. In season, it's a floral extravaganza. But look to the skies as well, for seeing the talkative deer might be topped by the flyover, complete with acrobatics, of a golden eagle.

There are only two trail junctions. Go right at the first (5,200 feet) and also right at the second (5,500 feet) at the **3.0**-mile mark. The ridge crest is reached in another 0.4 mile at 6,000 feet, yielding the first views westward into the heart of the range.

From here, a 20-minute stroll north along the rounded ridgetop leads to the summit rocks (6,280 feet), **4.1** scintillating miles from the trailhead. Note that the established trail actually bypasses the summit on its west side, so look for a side path on the right that leads up to the rocky summit area. If the ground is white, just head upward.

What more can be said of views that have become increasingly magnificent the whole way up? Even Mount Rainier shows itself midway along the final switchbacks below the top of the ridge. Out to the northwest, the Strait of Juan de Fuca can be seen near Port Angeles. Looking east over falling-away hills, catch the gleam off the waters of Hood Canal. Southeast, the canal view is blocked by the majesty of Mount Walker (Hike 56), another wonderful winter outing.

56 JEFFERSON COUNTY
Mount Walker

Distance:	6.2 miles round-trip
Time:	4 hours
Starting elevation:	780 feet
High point:	2,804 feet
Trail type:	Forest trail
Avalanche potential:	None
Difficulty level:	Strenuous
Map:	Pargeter's Revised Pictorial Map of the Olympic Mountains and/or USGS Mount Walker (7.5' series)

The Hike

If Mount Walker had tried any harder to be the easternmost sentry in the Olympic front, it would have wound up being yet another magnificent island in the greater Puget Sound archipelago. Sitting prominently on the shore of Dabob Bay, the mountain has both a driving road and a trail to its two observation points. Why not walk it and drive it, too?

Getting There

Summit Road is an east turn off U.S. 101 very close to milepost 300. The turn is 5 miles south of Quilcene.

Reset your odometer at the start of the viewpoint road. On the way to the summit, the road winds along the north flank of the mountain and nearly circles its top before reaching a T at 4.0 miles, 2,760 feet in elevation. Follow the sign left at that point to reach parking for the North Summit Observation Point at 4.2 miles, 2,804 feet, or go right for parking at the South Summit Observation Point at 4.4 miles. Walks from parking to viewing are short in both cases.

For the trail, drive the Mount Walker Viewpoint Road just 0.3 mile to the trailhead. There is lots of parking on the left side of the road.

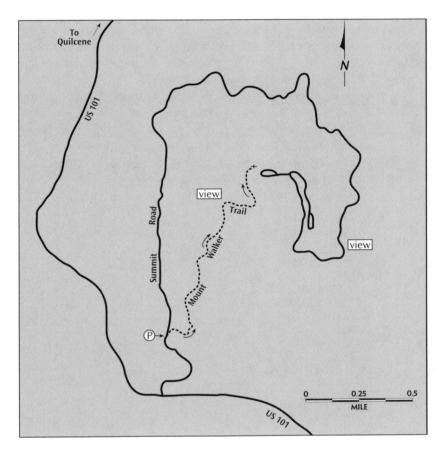

The Trail

The trail leaves on the right (east) side of the roadway across from the graveled parking area. It begins climbing steeply almost from the first toehold. It is a bit gravelly in places, but long sections are carpeted with the honey-brown of yesterday's needles.

At 1,500 feet or so, begin to catch glimpses of the country southward down Hood Canal. At 2,400 feet, **1.5** miles up, find a 20-foot-long side path to the left off a switchback that leads onto a knobby ledge with previews of the high mountains to the west. Back on the way up, the trail continues southeasterly onto the side of a plunging wooded ravine before swinging away to the north for the final stretch to North Summit.

Step up to the rail for a 180-degree, supervertical vista that runs from Mount Constance in the west to well south of Mount Baker in the northeast. In between are the Warrior Peaks (7,300-footers) and Mounts Buckhorn and Townsend. Below are both the town and the bay called Quilcene.

For more, walk 0.6 mile of road to the South Summit Observation Point. On the way, pass the right turn that is the Summit Road coming up from U.S. 101. Walk the loop trail to viewpoints, and spend what is left of your mind gazing raptly out over the Kitsap water world. No wonder much of the early settlement of the peninsula was accomplished by boat.

If the day is clear and you have hiked the trail, why not walk down the road for a different slant on things?

57 | Webb P

🥾🥾

Distance:	0.6 mile round-
Time:	1 hour
Starting elevation:	2,350 feet
High point:	2,775 feet
Trail type:	Old forest road
Avalanche potential:	None
Difficulty level:	Easy
Maps:	Hood Canal District Forest Ser
	and Pargeter's Revised Pictorial
	the Olympic Mountains

The Hike

Webb Point is, of course, lookoutless, as are most places with the "L.O." designation. No matter. It's a cutie. The peak's appeal may be that most of us do not even know it is there.

Getting There

Drive U.S. 101 to Hamma Hamma Recreation Road, Forest Road 25, at milepost 317.9, and turn west for 2.5 miles. At that point, turn right (north) on FR 2510, now gaining elevation. At 8.7 miles, reach a junction with FR 090. Turn left onto FR 090 for 1.0 mile to a prominent parking area on a sharp bend pointing northeast. Effectively, the road ends here, for it is deeply ditched and bermed after the curve.

A note of warning about FR 090: It has lots of very angular rocks on its surface that have ruined four-ply tires. It's a short hike. Why not walk it?

The Trail

It is difficult to find the trail for Webb Point without the reference of first going to the easily located berm and parking area on FR 090. From there, backtrack 0.1 mile and look on the right for the only place where an old road could be located. All else is steeply ascending embankment. There is no trail sign right there, but there is, coincidentally, a brown plastic FR 090 marker. A little poking around the young alders reveals a grassy berm, and then, 30 feet

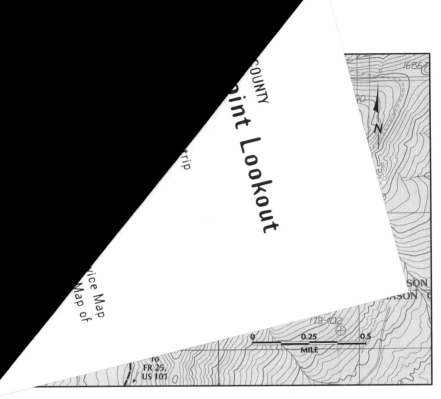

or so in on what is now plainly an old road returning to nature, are a pair of 6-inch-by-6-inch posts set 8 feet apart.

From there to the top, **0.3** mile, the way is never again in doubt. The view to the west and Mount Constance is magnificent, as any sighting of that landmark surely must be, and the eye may roam southward down Hood Canal all the way to Big Bend. Trees, in all their splendor, hide whatever vistas spread to the east and north.

This summit is a great place to camp, but bring water. There is solitude in abundance on site.

MASON COUNTY
58 | Jefferson Ridge

Distance: 3.8 miles round-trip
Time: 3.5 hours
Starting elevation: 2,200 feet
High point: 3,825 feet
Trail type: Forest trail
Avalanche potential: Slight
Difficulty level: Strenuous
Maps: USGS Mount Washington and USGS Eldon (7.5' series)

The Hike

Soaring skylines, plunging ridges, and nothing but air and distance: That's from the access road. Wait until you get to the trail. Both road and trail are steep and contorted, never able to wander far due to the increasing narrowness of the long ridge. The Jefferson Ridge Trail must be one of the backbones of heaven, for in late May it is strewn with wild rhododendron blossoms as if heralding one's approach to the pearly gates.

Getting There

Drive U.S. 101 to the Hamma Hamma Recreation Area entrance, Forest Road 25 at milepost 317.9, and turn west. At 6.4 miles, just past the Hamma Hamma Campground, turn left (south) onto FR 2480. At 6.7 miles the road splits at a sharp Y. Turn right onto FR 2421. Drive upward steeply to park at the trailhead at 9.7 miles (2,200 feet).

The Trail

"Up" is more than a general term here, meaning never extreme, but often your feet may want to explore for a little more bite on the somewhat gravelly texture of the trail. Almost immediately, and for two-thirds of the way, the route is in massive clear-cut.

At **0.8** mile (2,930 feet), the track intersects and crosses the same road that continues from the trailhead below. (It is gated about a half mile before the trail crossing.) After crossing the road, the track enters young plantation trees.

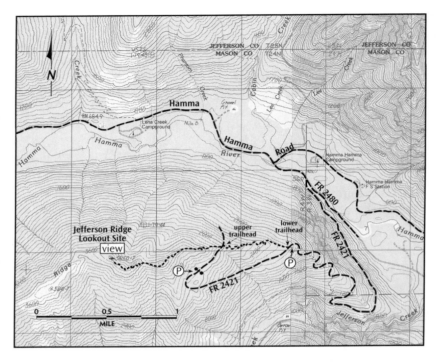

The ridge narrows while the views widen at windows along the way. There is respite from the relentless ascent at 3,380 feet, **1.1** miles up, where the trail pads along the flattened top of one of the backbone's vertebrae: relief with stunning panoramas.

The route is still in clear-cut until the **1.7**-mile point (3,650 feet), where it enters mature timber for the final push. Now it's up and down the humps and bumps. After a couple of switchbacks and one final rise, the trail ends at an old tent platform at the remains of the lookout at the top of Jefferson Ridge, **1.9** miles from the trailhead.

Views from the top are nothing compared to those below on the sheer-sided ridge, but the whole ascent is so exhilarating one simply must go to the top or be cheated.

59 | MASON COUNTY
Mount Rose

Distance: 6.3 miles round-trip
Time: 5 hours
Starting elevation: 800 feet
High point: 4,301 feet
Trail type: Forest trail to summit
Avalanche potential: None
Difficulty level: Strenuous
Maps: Custom Correct Mount Skokomish–Lake Cushman or Green Trails Mount Steel No. 167 and Mount Tebo No. 199

Down Lake Cushman to Hood Canal, from Mount Rose.

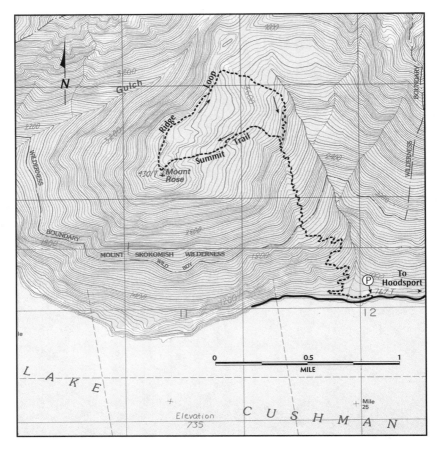

The Hike

By any other name, this one's still a beauty. But roses do have thorns, and this lady has a pip. Her trail is *stee-eep!* Mount Rose graces the north shore of Lake Cushman at its western extreme. In fact, it is the last landform in the national forest before its boundary with Olympic National Park.

Judging by lots of flagging tape hanging about 12 feet over the trail, the climbing of Mount Rose has to be carefully timed. Plan to do Mount Rose before December or after April 1.

Getting There

From the south, drive U.S. 101 to milepost 331.7, town center of Hoodsport, and turn west on Lake Cushman–Staircase Road. Drive to a stop sign at a T, 9.3 miles from U.S. 101. Turn left (west), still on Lake Cushman–Staircase Road. At 12.1 miles from U.S. 101, locate the trailhead access road for Mount Rose on the right. There is some parking 0.2 mile up the access road where the trail begins, but lots more along wide shoulders of Lake Cushman–Staircase Road.

The Trail

This trail is the put-the-head-down-and-chug kind of steep: never extreme, but rarely does it let up.

At **2.0** miles (3,000 feet) the trail splits. Left goes directly to the summit in 1.2 miles, while the right fork goes to the same place in 1.5 miles. There is a much larger difference, though, than what is represented by that three tenths of a mile. The Summit Trail climbs steeply most of the way to the top, but the right fork, the Ridge Loop Trail, climbs steeply only for half of its 1.5 miles. After it reaches the thin connecting ridge with Mount Ellinor, it rises only 400 feet in the second half, the three quarters of a mile along the scenic ridge.

One plan is to take the Summit Trail on the way up, and to descend the longer, somewhat easier Ridge Loop Trail to reduce the pounding on your feet and knees. However you do it, at least walk both choices.

The summit of Mount Rose, and likely a whole lot more of the mountain, is an excellent example of pillow lava. Tall columns of puffy-looking basalt stand just beneath the summit block and are very photogenic. So, too, is the scenery. In spite of its drowned river origin, Lake Cushman is a place of beauty. The imposing peaks to the southwest are Timber Mountain (242 degrees) and Lightning Peak (251 degrees). Behind Timber, but nearly 400 feet taller, is Dry Mountain. Obviously, someone forgot the water bottle on that one.

Coming up the Summit Trail, and also along the crest portion of the Ridge Loop Trail, are good views of Mount Ellinor to the northeast. Mount Rose's close neighbor, Copper Mountain, can be seen to the northwest during much of the traverse of the ridge.

60 | MASON COUNTY
South Mountain

Distance:	9.6 miles round-trip
Time:	6 hours
Starting elevation:	624 feet
High point:	3,070 feet
Trail type:	Forest roads
Avalanche potential:	Slight
Difficulty level:	Moderate to strenuous
Maps:	USGS Dry Bed Lakes and USGS Vance Creek (7.5' series) or Hood Canal Ranger District topo

East Summit of South Mountain, taken from the main summit.

The Hike

South Mountain? What a blah tag for a bully summit! But it is descriptive, for South Mountain is about as far in that direction as any of the Olympic peaks seem to be.

Getting There

Drive U.S. 101 to milepost 39.5, approximately 8.0 miles north of Shelton and 0.5 mile south of where the Skokomish River passes under the highway. Turn west on Skokomish Valley Road (not Skokomish River Road) and reset your odometer.

Go 5.6 miles to a right turn (northwest) onto Forest Road 23. After a sharp bend in FR 23 at 8.2 miles, turn left on unsigned FR 2341. Two things distinguish the turn: A bright orange gate, hopefully open, and gravel-surfaced FR 23 suddenly becoming paved. The route loses no time in dropping about 400 feet to cross Vance Creek.

At 11.4 miles, ignore unsigned FR 2342 on the right (north) side of the road.

At 12.8 miles, stay with FR 2341 as it goes right (west) at a T junction. (Bingham Creek flows beneath the intersection.)

At 15.1 miles from U.S. 101, look for a road (north) situated at 624 feet and at the western end of yet one more large clear-cut. And, holy heralds! Is that a real sign we see? It is small, ancient, short on eloquence, and half hidden in brush, but it does say, "SO MTN 820." Park here, or joyously take the road as far up as road conditions and weather permit. On the survey outing, the way was badly washed out at 1.4 miles, 1,640 feet in elevation. Carry and plod, but isn't that why we come?

The Trail

Ignore a possible left turn in the first **0.75** mile up. Leaving the washouts at the **1.4**-mile mark, the road trends west, then soon makes a great bend back to the east via a thin connecting ridge.

The whole area is characterized by very steep terrain and loose soils. Good luck, Earth, for along with that pair of erosion bell-ringers, the megaclear-cutting is strike three. Landslide scars are numerous.

Nice vistas appear at 2,240 feet. Another great bend brings the hiker to a saddle at **2.2** miles (2,350 feet). The area has been widely bulldozed, possibly to permit the turning around of logging rigs. From here, the communications towers and antennas of East Summit are visible.

At 2,660 feet the gradient slacks off, then flattens until a more definitive saddle is reached (2,800 feet) at the **4.4**-mile point. This saddle separates East Summit from the main summit. A very rough-looking road rises eastward from the saddle, presumably on its way to East Summit, but we did not follow it. Instead, go sharply left (west) toward South Mountain.

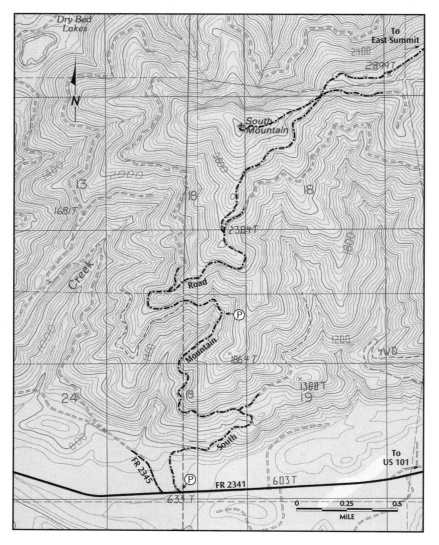

Though there are another 270 vertical feet to go, it is wowing time nonetheless, for three volcanoes are seen to the east and southeast. Squint, peer, and jump about, then go to the top, steeply once more.

Such a summit! South Mountain's tiny top once held an 8-foot-by-8-foot penthouse (lookout) with a similar-size front yard and little more, except its undiminished 360-degree view.

Start the parade from north to south with a pair of relative locals to the northeast, Mount Constance (21 degrees) and Mount Walker, up near Quilcene (35 degrees), followed by five volcanoes: Baker (37 degrees), Glacier Peak (62 degrees), Rainier (110 degrees), Adams (130 degrees), and St. Helens (143 degrees). The bonus, as well as the sixth volcano, is Mount Hood, an always dramatic spire, at 154 degrees from South Mountain. Awesome, awesome.

Apparently there's steel in the ground here. Take compass sightings from atop the big stump below the summit and 15 or 18 feet away from the old foundation.

Resources

Topographic Map Sources

USGS, Green Trails, and Custom Correct maps are available at most outdoor stores. Or order them from:

USGS

Earth Sciences Center
135 U.S. Post Office, 904 W. Riverside Avenue Spokane, WA 99201   509-353-2524

Metsker Maps
702 First Avenue, Seattle, WA 98104   206-623-8747
14150 NE 20th Street, Bellevue, WA 98007   425-746-3200
6249 Tacoma Mall Blvd., Tacoma, WA 98409   253-474-6277

Custom Correct Maps (Olympic Peninsula trail maps)

Little River Enterprises
3492 Little River Road, Port Angeles, WA 98363   360-457-5667

National Forest Service Maps

NFS maps are available at some outdoor stores. Or order them from:

Darrington Ranger District
1405 Emmens Street, Darrington, WA 98241   360-436-1155

Skykomish Ranger District
74920 NE Stevens Pass Hwy , Skykomish, WA 98288   360-677-2414

Glacier Public Service Ctr.
1094 Mt. Baker Hwy, Glacier, WA 98244   360-599-2714

Verlot Public Service Ctr. (summer only)
33515 Mountain Loop Hwy, Granite Falls, WA 98252   360-691-7791

Mt. Baker Ranger District
2105 Hwy 20. Sedro Woolley, WA 98284   360-856-5700
(ext. 515 for trail reports)

Hood Canal Ranger District
P.O. Box 68, N. 150 Lake Cushman Road, Hoodsport, WA 98548   360-877-5254

Quilcene Ranger District
P.O. Box 280, 20482 Hwy 101, Quilcene, WA 98376   360-765-2200

Specialty Maps

Pargeter's Pictorial Maps
Excellent for mileages, forest road numbers, and area view. Available at most outdoor stores. Three maps: North Cascades Central, North Cascades West, and Olympic Mountains.

Washington Atlas & Gazetteer
Available in bookstores and outdoor stores. Published by DeLorme.

Road Maps
When hiking destinations are more rural than wild, a good road map may be more help than a topographic product.

King of the Road Maps
Include county road maps and maps of areas such as Whidbey Island and the San Juan Islands. Available at Fred Meyer and Safeway as well as at gas stations, convenience stores, book shops, and outdoor stores.

Free San Juan Islands road maps

For Lopez Island:
Lopez Chamber of Commerce, P.O. Box 102, Lopez Island, WA 98261   360-378-2240

For San Juan Island:
San Juan Island National Historic Park, P.O. Box 429, Friday Harbor, WA 98250

Special Trail Maps

For Mt. Constitution:
Moran State Park, Star Route, Box 22, Eastsound, WA 98245   360-676-2326

For Mt. Erie and Whistle Lake:
ACFL Office, P.O. Box 547, Anacortes, WA 98221

Important Phone Numbers
Crown Pacific forest land entry permit: 360-826-3002
Avalanche hazard, Cascades and Olympics: 206-526-6677
Public road information: 206-455-7900
National Weather Service Forecast: 206-526-6087

Books (on compass, altimeter, and Global Positioning System use)
Staying Found, 2nd ed., by June Fleming. Seattle: Mountaineers Books, 1994.
GPS Land Navigation, by Michael Ferguson. Boise: Glassford Publishing, 1997.